GREENE & GREENE
THE BLACKER HOUSE

GREENE & GREENE
THE BLACKER HOUSE

RANDELL L. MAKINSON

THOMAS A. HEINZ

with a photographic essay by BRAD PITT

Entry hall stairway railing, featuring
finger-lap joinery and ebony
square-peg detail.

GIBBS·SMITH
P
PUBLISHER

SALT LAKE CITY

DEDICATION

To Ellen and Harvey Knell,

for their preservation and faithful restoration of the

Robert R. Blacker House,

thereby providing for ongoing generations

a better understanding of our national architectural heritage,

the genius of architects Greene & Greene,

and the ideals of the

Arts & Crafts movement in America.

Subtle patterns of lotus leaves, imagery from the lake outside, were carried out in gesso relief with gold-leaf overlay in the living room frieze.

First Edition

05 04 03 02 01 00   5 4 3 2 1

Published by
Gibbs Smith, Publisher
P.O. Box 667
Layton, Utah 84041

Web site: www.gibbs-smith.com
Orders, toll free: (800) 748-5439

Design by Randell L. Makinson and
Thomas A. Heinz

Printed and bound in Hong Kong

**Library of Congress Cataloging-
in-Publication Data**

Makinson, Randell L., 1932-
   Greene & Greene : the Blacker
   House / by Randell L. Makinson,
   Thomas A. Heinz, with a photographic
   essay by Brad Pitt—1st ed.
   p. cm.
   ISBN 0-87905-949-4
1. Robert Roe Blacker House
(Pasadena, Calif.) 2. Blacker, Robert
Roe, 1845–1931.—Homes and
haunts—California—Pasadena.
3. Greene & Greene. 4. Pasadena
(Calif.)—Buildings, structures, etc.
I. Heinz, Thomas A. II. Title.
   NA 7238.P26 M35 2000
   728.8'09794'93—dc21
   99-089918

CONTENTS

Living room lantern and gold-leaf detail on ceiling as photographed from the floor.

PREFACE

Split redwood shakes on the walls respond independently to the transparent Cabot's penetrating-oil stains, bringing life and vitality to the exterior of the house.

The restoration of the Blacker House in Pasadena, California, from 1994 to 1999, revealed for the first time in fifty years the original color, patina, and textures of Greene & Greene exteriors, and added considerable information about the building vocabulary that we identify as the Greene & Greene Style. At the same time, a close scrutiny of the Blacker House has posed new questions about the role of the client in the design, the importance of the Blacker and Canfield family heritages, and the various circumstances that ultimately resulted in the construction of the largest of the Greenes' highly articulated timber designs.

Over many years, seemingly unrelated events occurred that gave direction to the planning and construction of the Robert R. Blacker House (1907). The physical embodiment of these situations has established it as one of the masterworks of American architects Greene & Greene. That it was built at all is an extraordinary feat: the floor plan was by another architect, there were two separate general contractors responsible for the construction work, the Blackers lived in another house on the 5.1-acre site during the construction of the main house, and additions and alterations to the several buildings and the estate were carried out over two decades. In spite of many complications, this international landmark of craftsmanship and the Arts & Crafts movement stood proudly among its neighbors only as long as it remained in Blacker ownership.

Following Nellie Blacker's death on 22 May 1944, the property was subdivided by new owners. From the Blacker House, furniture was sold, and, over time, neglect, alterations, and ill-advised maintenance depleted the original integrity of the design, contributing to the destabilization of neighborhood property values. Later, the overnight removal of the original lighting fixtures and art glass was a final indignity that spurred the discussion and led to the enactment of legislation in many parts of the country to protect a community's architectural heritage from scavenging encouraged by outside speculative interests.

Over the years, the original finishes and colorations that gave dignity and integrity to each of the construction materials of the house had turned black. Dry rot and weathering had eaten away at structural members; some were missing and others left hanging.

Once the flagship of the Oak Knoll subdivision, the Blacker House had become the eyesore. At one time, it had nearly been dismantled. Fortunately, in 1994 the house was purchased by sympathetic owners who appreciated its architectural merits. Because of their enlightened vision, the Blacker House stands today as a monument to the genius of its youthful and innovative architects and entourage of master craftsmen.

With the purchase of the remaining property by Ellen and Harvey Knell in 1994, the Blacker House has undergone a meticulous restoration. The Knells assembled a new team of master craftsmen who matched the high standards that Charles and Henry Greene had set for themselves and their workmen. This achievement has had an important impact on other Greene & Greene owners. Several restoration projects are now in process, and the full restoration of Charles Greene's personal residence and studio in Pasadena has been completed.

The experience gained from the restoration of the Blacker House demonstrated that a knowledge of the background and activities of the original owners was essential to an understanding of the final design of the house, its furnishings, artifacts, and grounds. This naturally led to an in-depth study of Robert Roe Blacker and Nellie Canfield Blacker, their activities and houses in Manistee, Michigan, and Robert's origins in Brantford, Ontario, Canada.

The authors' trips to Manistee and Brantford produced valuable records, documents, and archival photographs. New photographs were taken of the Blacker houses and related imagery. Information gained from these trips has resulted in the depth and detail given in the Introduction. The Blackers' move to Pasadena, the selection of the site, the design for the house by Myron Hunt and Elmer Grey, and the switch to architects Greene & Greene are addressed in the first chapter. The Greene & Greene design, construction, various Greene & Greene additions, development of the site, analysis of the plan, and a review of the archival photographs are dealt with in following chapters. Other works by Greene & Greene and associated with the Blackers, including the Annie Blacker House in Pasadena, the cottage and two bungalows in

Long Beach, the bungalow in Santa Monica, and the William R. Thorsen House in Berkeley, are discussed chronologically. The quantity and significance of the Greene & Greene decorative arts and furniture designed expressly for the Blacker House are dealt with independently.

Brad Pitt's passion for fine architecture, his extensive knowledge of the architecture and decorative arts of the international Arts & Crafts movement, and his intense respect for the work of Greene & Greene are reflected through his camera lens in a photographic essay devoted to his personal images and impressions of the house.

The subdivision of the property, the sale of the furnishings, and the public outrage over the stripping of the lighting fixtures and windows from the house is addressed in a separate chapter.

Concluding this study is a discussion of the meticulous restoration of the Blacker House and its furnishings. Its present owners indeed rescued the international landmark and have breathed new life into its presence. Their sensitive and thoughtful approach to the work has provided a meaningful gift to the architectural heritage of this nation, not only by their acts but also by their generosity in sharing their experience in various ways with the broader architectural community.

This monograph is a joint collaboration of two authors in the research, photography, writing, and design made possible by a friendship of more than twenty-five years and enhanced by the enthusiasm that Brad Pitt shares for the restoration of the Blacker House.

Randell L. Makinson, Hon. AIA, Pasadena, California
Thomas A. Heinz, AIA, Evanston, Illinois

Dining room plate rails and the intra-house telephone were carefully coordinated with the dark mahogany paneling of the walls and the square-peg joinery.

The Grand River, twisting through Brantford, Ontario, Canada, continues to be the lifeline of the community. Photographed from the Blacker Mount Pleasant house and site of the former Blacker brickyard.

INTRODUCTION

The former Blacker farm in Brantford, Ontario, Canada.

A study of the Robert Roe Blacker House in Pasadena must include historical and biographical information about Blacker's life in Canada and Michigan and about the Blacker, Canfield, and Thorsen families. The Blacker family arrived in Ontario in the early 1800s, the Thorsen family in Philadelphia in 1820, and the Canfields in Milford, Connecticut, as early as 1646. When the first Blacker—Robert's grandfather, Edward—arrived in Brantford, fewer than a dozen Europeans lived in the area, making him one of the pioneers in the region. Over sixty years after the Blackers established themselves and their brick-manufacturing facilities, Ontario became one of the first four provinces of Canada when it was founded on 1 July 1867.

The Blacker Family

The Blacker and the Greene family trees were rooted in central Britain, in Yorkshire and the Lake District, respectively. Blacker's grandfather, Edward Blacker, and his wife, Mary Roe, immigrated to Canada from Yorkshire in the late 1700s. They stayed first in Hamilton, Ontario, at the west end of Lake Ontario, before settling in Brantford, initially as farmers and then as brick manufacturers. Here Edward purchased thirty acres of farmland along the Tutela Heights Road on the bluffs overlooking the city of Brantford. The rest of the family remained in England.

Brantford, Ontario

Brantford was one of the industrial centers in what was then known as Upper Canada. It was already known as a center for agricultural implements and finance. Robert Blacker's father, Edward, was born in 1806. His grandmother, Mary Roe, died in 1807, her husband in 1815, and both were buried in the Farringdon Burial Ground in Brantford. Fifteen years later, at the age of twenty-six, Robert's father participated in the Mackenzie Rebellion and became a warm personal friend of William Lyon Mackenzie. For several generations, Blacker family members were active in politics and political movements.

Edward returned to the farm in Brantford and around 1840 married Margaret Tomlinson, who had emigrated from Manchester, England. Their family of six children began in 1842 with the birth of John, followed by Edward in 1844, Robert Roe

Blacker on 31 October 1845, Mary in 1847, Ann (Annie) in 1848, and William in 1850. Robert's older brother John established his own business in building products on the south edge of the town. Little is known of Robert's brother Edward. Mary and Annie, both spinsters, remained close to all the brothers. William took over the operation of the family brick business when his father turned it over to him and Robert in 1879.

Blacker Brick

In 1836, at the age of thirty-one, Robert's father, Edward, had established the first of the Blacker Brick manufacturing businesses by taking over the Calvin Houghton brickyard, which had been operating since 1833 at the corner of Colborne Street and Stanley Avenue, near the eastern border of Brantford. The Blacker brick business flourished, and in 1842, three years before Robert's birth, his father opened a second brick manufacturing operation south of town on the Grand River landing site on the road to Newport. In 1853, he and Margaret bought a farm of 130 acres, establishing yet another brick operation there. This land, however, did not contain enough clay for long-term production, and the brick-making activity was soon shut down.

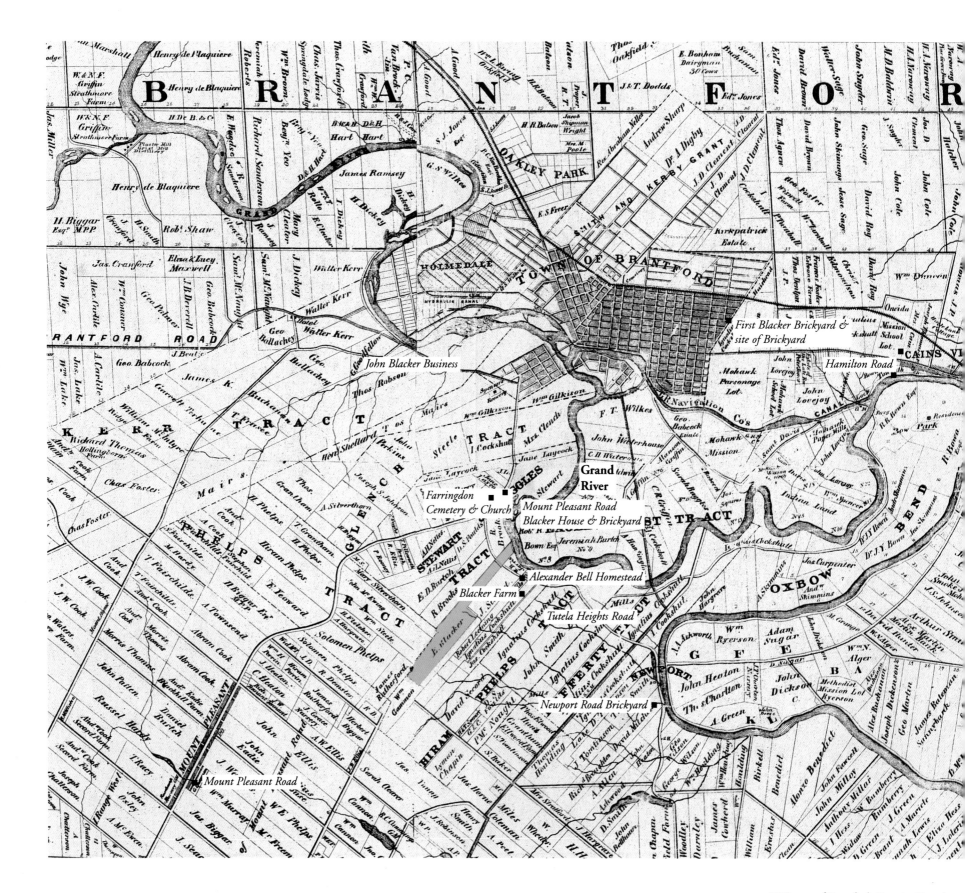

First Blacker Brickyard & site of Brickyard

Hamilton Road

John Blacker Business

Grand River

Farringdon Cemetery & Church

Mount Pleasant Road
Blacker House & Brickyard

Alexander Bell Homestead

Blacker Farm

Tutela Heights Road

Newport Road Brickyard

Mount Pleasant Road

1858 map of Brantford, Ontario, Canada

2

Top: Typical Brantford house
constructed of Blacker yellow brick.

Middle: Brick detail in Blacker red
brick.

Robert Blacker purchased the final location of the Blacker
brickyard in 1877. It fronted on Mount Pleasant Road, a mile
south of the Brantford city limits and across from the Farringdon
Church and Cemetery, and it backed up to the west bank of the
Grand River. The property contained a small two-story brick
house, possibly dating as early as 1840 but with later additions.
On this land, the brickyard established in 1879 became the largest
in Ontario. It produced over 2.5 million bricks per year, using
wood for fuel and running three steam-operated Townley Stock
Brick Machines with a daily output of four thousand bricks each.
In the 1880s, the yard employed twenty-six men and boys.

Brantford remains a small city of beautiful old brick buildings,
both commercial and residential. According to local lore, many
masons who were highly skilled emigrated from England and
brought with them the late Victorian styles. The Blacker brick
operations were major contributors to the beauty of the city, and
even today there is a premium on what are termed "Golden
Bricks," those that were manufactured by the Blackers.

The Blacker Brantford Houses

The first Blacker house in Brantford (ca. 1805) cannot be
identified because of the lack of early records, but it was probably
in the city proper, as the first brickyard was on the east edge of the
city limits. The second Blacker house was set back from the road
and the Grand River. Directly across from the Blacker farmhouse,
Alexander Melville Bell, father of Alexander Graham Bell, bought
a part of the Blacker farm. The Bell homestead was situated
between the Tutela Heights Road and the Grand River. During his
summer vacation in 1874, young Alexander confounded his
neighbors by stringing wires around the neighborhood, developing
and testing his invention of the telephone. Diaries within the
Blacker family recall the historic event and comment that the
neighbors thought the young Alexander was "nuts." Letters extant
between the inventor and his mother frequently discuss the
Blacker family, who were often the Bells' dinner guests. The
120-acre Tutela Heights farm exists today with little change.
According to family letters, the Blacker farmhouse burned shortly
after 1900 and the property was sold to the Andrew Hird family
in 1911.

Blacker Brothers Brickyards

In 1879, Robert's father, Edward, turned the brick business over
to two of his sons, Robert and William. At the time, thirty-four-
year-old Robert was already established with his lumber interests
in Michigan and, while retaining his interest in the brick
operations in Brantford, turned the entire day-to-day operation
over to William. Blacker brick became recognized for its quality.
Under William's leadership, each brick was impressed with the
words "B Bros." in the recess. The Blacker Brothers Brickyard
was the only manufacturing facility in Canada producing both
yellow and red brick, the red being pressed in both a light and
a dark shade.

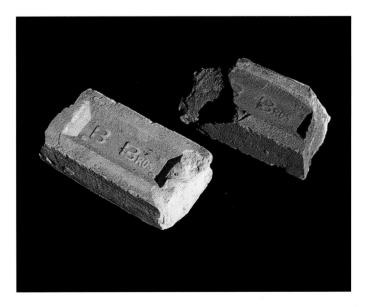

Blacker Brothers bricks were made in red
and yellow and marked "B Bros."

The last Blacker house in Brantford was on the Mount Pleasant Road property around the corner and over a half mile from the Tutela Heights farm. It stands today very much as it did when it was first acquired by the Blackers in the late 1870s. After the Blacker family sold the house in 1958, two small additions were made, one to the south side and another over the entry portico. The property is now smaller as a result of a recent subdivision. The brickyard is long gone and several barns have either been demolished or relocated.

Around the turn of the century, one of the family who was visiting relatives in England purchased a handsomely carved dining room cabinet, shipped it to Brantford, and brought along English cabinetmakers who installed it in the dining room.

The Brantford house remained in the Blacker family, although under different family ownerships, until the death of Robert Blacker's nephew, Edward Miles (Miley) Blacker, in 1958. Robert sold the Mount Pleasant home to the Blacker Brick Company in 1879. In 1905, it was purchased from the Blacker Brick Company by his sister, Annie Blacker, who kept it as a house for her siblings and her nephew, Miles, son of her oldest brother, John, and his wife, Mary Coleman Blacker. On Annie's death in 1926, it reverted jointly to her sister, Mary, and to Miles, and in 1929, after Mary's death, to Miles. When Miles died in 1958, this historic house was acquired by David and Ruth Bryant. It was finally purchased by George and Lorraine Skitch, who today fill the house with memorabilia of those members of the Blacker family who had built and cared for it for nearly a century.

The Fenian Raids

In 1864, Robert Roe Blacker, who was then nineteen years old, left the farm to work as a laborer in the lumber camps in Buchanan, Michigan, but returned to Brantford two years later to deal with the threat of the Irish-American Fenians. He joined the brigade from Brantford along with other young men from the town who had been working in the United States. The experience, according to Robert in a *Brantford Expositer* news interview at his Pasadena home in 1928, was a turning point in his life. "When I returned to the farm [on Tutela Heights Road] I had seen more of the world, and having had that taste, I decided a little later to launch out on my own account. If it hadn't been for those Fenians, I would probably be on the farm yet." So he stated, although he had left the farm two years earlier for the lumber camps in Buchanan.

Former Blacker house on Mount Pleasant Road, Brantford, as it appears today.

At that time, a lumberman or lumberjack worked during the winter on a seasonal basis. Logs were cut and loaded on large sleds pulled by the biggest horses—Percherons—that could pull such a heavy load to the frozen river. When he went back to the lumber camp following the Fenian Raids, Robert impressed his superiors with his logical mind. Robert also had the knowledge and experience of his duties at his father's brickyard operations. He was good with numbers and had a retentive memory, two qualities necessary for a lumber inspector's job, a position normally occupied by older and more experienced lumbermen. These inspectors were very important and had to be extremely accurate in their estimates. They were required to be expert in the identification of the species of each and every log and to judge the quality and yield, in board feet, of each given log. Profits depended on the expertise of the inspectors, who were regulated by the lumber industry leaders in Chicago. That Robert should have been accorded such a responsible position at the young age of twenty-one was extraordinary. The reasons why he went to Buchanan in the first place are puzzling. However, Buchanan was on the direct route between Brantford and Chicago. It was a lumber town. While one of the principal founders of Buchanan in the 1830s was a man by the name of John M. Roe, and many prominent positions in Buchanan were held by members of the Roe family, there is no evidence to date indicating that this Roe family had any connection to that of Robert's paternal grandmother, Mary Roe.

Mount Pleasant Road house dining room and niche, with cabinetwork the Blackers had shipped from England.

Manistee, Michigan

Following Robert Blacker's brief years in Buchanan, he relocated to Manistee, Michigan, where he resided throughout his active professional life in the lumber industry.

Manistee is on the eastern shore of Lake Michigan, about halfway between Chicago and Mackinac. A small river runs through the town, connecting the shallow, five-mile-long Lake Manistee on the east with Lake Michigan on the west, thus creating a natural port. Since the smaller lake completely freezes over, moving lumber by horse and sled is much easier in winter.

John and Joseph Stronach, the first white settlers, landed in Manistee in 1841 and made arrangements with the Chippewa Indians to set up a sawmill. A few years later, in 1849, John Canfield, son of a lumberman from Racine, Wisconsin, arrived and set up his sawmill at the mouth of the Manistee River. Manistee's population grew to 1,000 in 1860, and when Robert arrived from Buchanan in 1866, he found a bustling lumber town where whiskey was heartily consumed and bare-fisted street fighting was common. In October 1871, a great fire broke out in Manistee and several cities surrounding Lake Michigan, including Peshtigo, Wisconsin, as well as Chicago. The downtown Manistee area was spared but the houses and woods all around the city burned. The citizens of Manistee helped repair the damage and were quick to give shelter to those in need.

Technological improvements soon after the fire included a telegraph line installed in 1872, and a year later Manistee had a population of 5,000. Over 300 boats a day took lumber to Racine, Milwaukee, Detroit, and Chicago. Well diggers from Chicago drilled for oil but discovered, instead, a twenty-five-foot-thick vein of salt below the city. At the same time, the first railroad reached town, providing land access to the rest of the country. The winters were warmer and summers cooler than in the rest of Michigan, and this, coupled with the sandy loam soil, was ideal for growing all types of fruit. Today Manistee is the fruit center of Michigan.

According to the 1870 census, Blacker rented a room above Mr. Shakelton's store in the business district, and in 1874, at the age of thirty, he entered into business with one of the most active entrepreneurs of west Michigan, Richard G. Peters. They operated a shingle mill, which produced 300,000 shingles a day, under the name of R. Blacker & Co. Blacker quickly expanded his business and on 4 April 1876 was appointed receiver of the assets of the

Davis & Co. shingle mill. Along with two partners, E. T. Davies and Patrick Noud, he opened a lumber mill as well as a shingle mill at the east end of Seventh Avenue on the west side of Lake Manistee, a key location. Noud was Blacker's age and also from Ontario. This operation, Davies, Blacker & Co., produced 16 million board feet of lumber and 20 million shingles per year. The plant was fully furnished with the latest sawdust chains and pulleys along with a special furnace feeder. On 2 April 1876, Noud and Blacker incorporated the State Lumber Company at the same location. Noud was president and Blacker secretary, treasurer, and general manager. The plant was on twenty-five acres on the west shore of Lake Manistee with direct access to the rail spurs of two railroads. In 1899, the State Lumber Company had sufficient land holdings in seven counties of Michigan with hemlock, cedar, and oak stands for at least fifteen years of cutting for the mill. It operated until 1910.

Archival overview drawing of Manistee, Michigan, showing location of Noud & Blacker's State Lumber Company.

State Lumber Company.

Right: Sanborn map of Robert Blacker's State Lumber Company.

Middle: Robert Roe Blacker

Far Right: Hattie Louise Williams Blacker

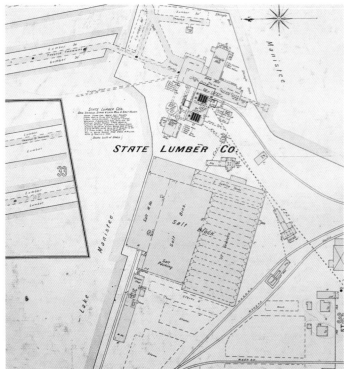

Lower right: Maple Street house (center), Manistee, Michigan.

Blacker's business interests were not limited to shingles and lumber. He had a position with two railroads: the Manistee & Grand Rapids Railway and the Manistee, Filer City & East Lake Railway, an electrically operated system. He was also active in two banks: Manistee County Savings Bank and the First National Bank of Manistee. Blacker was on the boards of the A. H. Lyman Wholesale Drug Company and the Manistee Water Works. These positions all required an individual with a keen business sense and constituted a range of operations that kept him in touch with the other major businessmen of Manistee in noncompetitive venues.

As if this were not too much for one person to handle, Blacker held several public offices. His first elected office was in 1882 to a seat in the state legislature. In 1884, he was a delegate to the Democratic National Convention when Grover Cleveland was put forth as a candidate and then elected president. In 1888, at forty-three years of age, he was appointed mayor of Manistee and served for four successive terms, until 1895. On 24 December 1891, Michigan Governor Edward B. Winans appointed Blacker to the position of secretary of state. In 1896, he was delegate-at-large to the Democratic Convention held in Chicago the year Democrat William Jennings Bryan lost to Republican William McKinley. Little is known of Blacker's interests outside of business. He married Harriet (Hattie) Williams, of Buchanan, on 2 February 1872 at her father's house in Buchanan, six years after he had left Buchanan for Manistee. They returned to Manistee after the wedding, and in 1875 he purchased a house at 111 Maple.

According to the 1880 census, they had a live-in servant, Mary Crane. The house was a small, 800-square-foot, story-and-a-half, gabled structure across the alley from the Ramsdell Theater on Maple. The Blackers lived there until the completion of their newly constructed house in 1892, on the southwest corner of Fifth and Oak Streets. The designer of the house was not reported in the local press, although three years later a large stable was built at the southwest corner of the lot and was designed by the prominent Chicago architectural firm Holabird & Roche. It is possible that this firm also designed the house, but no documents indicating this exist in the firm's archives.

The Oak Street house was a two-story wood-frame structure with horizontal shiplap siding. There is a large porch on the left side at the rear and a curved bay on the right front. The 3,000-square-foot multi-gabled house was certainly not among the largest in the neighborhood. The lot was perhaps a third of an acre. The composition was quiet, with neither frills nor ornaments such as brackets or grilles. There were no towers, turrets, circle windows, or pointed arches. It was a solid, compact design bordering on the clean modern look.

After more than ten years of marriage, it was apparent that the Blackers were not going to have children of their own. They adopted a daughter, according to the Manistee *Evening Times* of 19 May 1883, and also took the girl's younger brother. The two were named Alice Marie Simpson and Edward James Simpson. They had been born in 1878 and 1880 to Mary Knight Simpson of Brantford. Curiously, Alice was always considered a daughter and Edward a nephew.

On a summer day, 11 June 1896, Robert's wife, Hattie, was returning home in a carriage when it suddenly sped up. Thinking it a runaway, she jumped from the carriage, landing on her head and suffering severe injuries, and was taken home and soon joined by Robert. Two hours later she died. This was the biggest shock of Robert Blacker's life. The entire community grieved, as she was very well liked.

Alice Marie Simpson Blacker,
near eight years of age.

Edward James Simpson Blacker,
near two years of age.

Robert and Hattie Blacker Oak Street
house, Manistee, Michigan.

Right: Robert Roe Blacker, 1900.

Far right: Nellie Canfield Blacker, 1900.

Almost four years later, at age fifty-five, Robert married Nellie Canfield. The wedding took place on 22 February 1900 in a Grand Rapids ceremony. Nellie was the eldest daughter of John Canfield, who had come to Manistee in 1849 and set up a sawmill. Eventually, he became a banker, the owner of two of the biggest lumber mills in Manistee and clearly the most prominent citizen in town. His house, designed by Chicago architect William Le Baron Jenny, was the largest house in Manistee. The yard took up an entire block. Mr. Canfield died in 1899, leaving a son, Charles, and three daughters, Nellie, Caroline, and Ida.

John Canfield estate, Manistee, Michigan; William Le Baron Jenny, architect.

Caroline had married her father's partner, William R. Thorsen, and he, like his father-in-law, turned to Jenny as well for the design of his Manistee house. The three sisters were reported to be classmates of Mary Morris (Mrs. Charles Pratt) and Louise Gibbs (Mrs. David B. Gamble) at Vassar College in New York, each of whom in later years became clients of architects Greene & Greene.

Because of a change in the tax laws, Robert Blacker and his brother-in-law, Charles Canfield, mayor of Manistee, relocated to Chicago. As reported in the *Manistee Daily News* and the *Chicago Tribune* on 12 November 1900, Nellie and Robert departed Manistee for Chicago at the same time. The newspapers reported Canfield's Chicago address as 4305 South Grand Boulevard (now South Martin Luther King Drive). Blacker's address was listed as 418 48th Place, a few blocks south of the Canfields, off the corner of Grand Boulevard.

In searching the property records of these two locations, neither party was listed as owner at any time, and presumably both the Canfields and the Blackers were renting. Blacker sold his Manistee house to his sister, Annie, but was still listed as the resident in the Manistee city directories until the 1920s, when the property was sold out of the Blacker family. The move to Chicago seemed to be a move on paper instead of a physical one, as Blacker's and Canfield's residencies are never listed in the Chicago city directories. Although he apparently did not reside in Chicago, Blacker became active in a business venture and bought the Michigan Steamship Co., which was listed in the Chicago Directory. He replaced his partner, Noud, as president in 1903. The company was reorganized and consolidated with the Dunley–Williams group as the Chicago–South Haven Line and a year later, 1907, sold to a group of Cleveland investors for $150,000. A ship, the *Eastland,* owned by the Michigan Steamship Co., was constructed as a lake freighter in 1903 and piloted by Captain J. J. McKean, also a partner in the venture. After Blacker sold his interests, the *Eastland* was converted to passenger service and docked on the Chicago River across from the Merchandise Mart on Wacker Drive. In 1915 it suffered the worst maritime tragedy

in U.S. history. It was berthed on LaSalle Street to pick up Western Electric employees for an outing when a disturbance caused all on board to rush to one side of the boat. It capsized and 844 people drowned within a few feet of shore.

Chicago was the largest port served by Manistee. Blacker and most of the other Manistee businessmen must have made many trips by lake ferry and train over the years and were familiar with people and locations there. Blacker felt a need to establish himself in the city, and, in 1905, he applied for and was granted membership in the exclusive Chicago Athletic Club that was quartered in a large building at Michigan Avenue and Madison Street. Within the club were many athletic facilities, including squash courts and a beautiful tiled swimming pool. Stunning dining rooms of several sizes were available for large or small gatherings and were favorite locations for business meetings. Members included top Chicago executives, including Julius Rosenwald, head of Sears, Roebuck & Co., and Harold McCormick of International Harvester. Blacker's application was as a resident member. He listed his residence at the Auditorium Annex, located a few blocks south on Michigan Avenue and across from Adler and Sullivan's Auditorium Building. Blacker remained a lifelong member.

Robert Blacker was sixty years old in 1904. He had worked hard over the past forty years at a wide range of businesses, all focused around his lumber operations in Manistee. He served not only his own interests but also those of the citizenry through his many public offices, in all of which he demonstrated his organizational and leadership abilities. With the advent of a new century, the Blackers began to travel for pleasure and to enjoy the fruits of their labors.

William R. Thorsen House,
Manistee, Michigan; William
Le Baron Jenny, architect.

Robert R. Blacker in
Yokohama, Japan,
ca. 1905.

Robert and Nellie Blacker House,
Pasadena, California, 1999.

1

PASADENA

Robert and Nellie Blacker had become regular winter visitors at the Maryland Hotel in Pasadena shortly after the turn of the century. Both had lost loved ones: Nellie's father, John Canfield, the leading lumber baron in Manistee, had died in 1899 and Robert's first wife, Hattie, had been killed in a carriage accident in 1896. Moreover, Robert had recently focused his business interests in Chicago rather than Manistee, where he had spent most of his adult years in the lumber business. The move was prompted by an inequity of a new tax structure imposed on certain lumber interests, as well as the fact that the forests of Michigan had been played out. This last factor had caused his new brother-in-law, William R. Thorsen, to wrap up his lumber business in Manistee as well, and move first to Arizona and then to northern California. Thorsen was the husband of Nellie Blacker's sister, Caroline Canfield, who, shortly after the construction of the Blacker House in Pasadena, commissioned Greene & Greene to design the Thorsen House in the Berkeley Hills of northern California.

The Canfield sisters had grown up in a large mansion in Manistee and were accustomed to having extensive property with surrounding gardens and servants. The Canfields and the Blackers were business associates and competitors, who had known one another for many years when the spinster Nellie and the widowed Robert were married in 1900. And now Robert seemed to be ready in his own life to devote more time to his home, to his wife, and to a broader involvement with community affairs.

The Blackers likely began visiting Pasadena during the winter of 1901 after the wedding of Robert's adopted daughter, Alice Marie Simpson Blacker, to William Hallman Slingluff of Chicago. With his adopted son, Edward, in college, he and Nellie were now in a position to consider the future of their life together. In Pasadena the Blackers found the opportunity to enter a new and fulfilling part of their lives, with the time and the resources to combine and balance their individual interests in business, community, and philanthropy. Robert Blacker had retired from his active life in the lumber industry, though he would never step away completely.

The Maryland, like several other winter hotels in Pasadena, was frequented by guests as involved with national business concerns as Robert Blacker. Nellie Blacker found equally satisfying interests in attending the various artistic and theatrical events that had long been a part of the highly cultured social scene, and long after her moving into her own home, she served on committees at the hotel and was a patroness of theatrical benefits for the Children's Training School and other organizations.

The Maryland Hotel, located directly on Colorado Boulevard two blocks from the center of town, was the annual destination of many of the most active leaders in the area. It attracted a quality clientele by promoting itself in eastern newspapers. The hotel accommodated large parties and gave its guests a household feeling by offering large suites and a small "neighborhood" of bungalows, some designed by Myron Hunt. There were festivities that catered to the lifestyles of the guests, and occasionally the guests would host gatherings of friends and business associates. The hotel management tried to make it a home away from home for their guests who stayed for the winter season between November and April.

The 15 November 1906 issue of *Maryland Life,* a weekly publication of the hotel, reported: "Mr. and Mrs. R. R. Blacker of Chicago arrive within the next few days for their first visit of this season." A later account stated: "Mr. and Mrs. Blacker are warm friends of the Maryland, having been its guests for a long time. . . ."

Oak Knoll

Almost a year before the fashionable rolling virgin countryside of the Oak Knoll subdivision in southeast Pasadena was offered for public sale, the Blackers became aware of the property through their acquaintances at the Maryland, particularly the Huntingtons.

The gently rolling landscape of the Oak Knoll subdivision was first promoted as Oak Knoll Park in 1886, during Pasadena's first land boom. Not a single lot was sold. The land continued, undeveloped, as undulating pasture with majestic 200-year-old live oak trees and cool glens where sheep grazed the slopes. But the grand design of the Oak Knoll Park subdivision was most progressive. It followed the graceful curves of the swales and valleys in accordance with the philosophy of landscape architect Frederick Law Olmsted, who believed that street patterns should respond to the contours of the land.

Oak Knoll Ranch, Pasadena, ca. 1900.

14

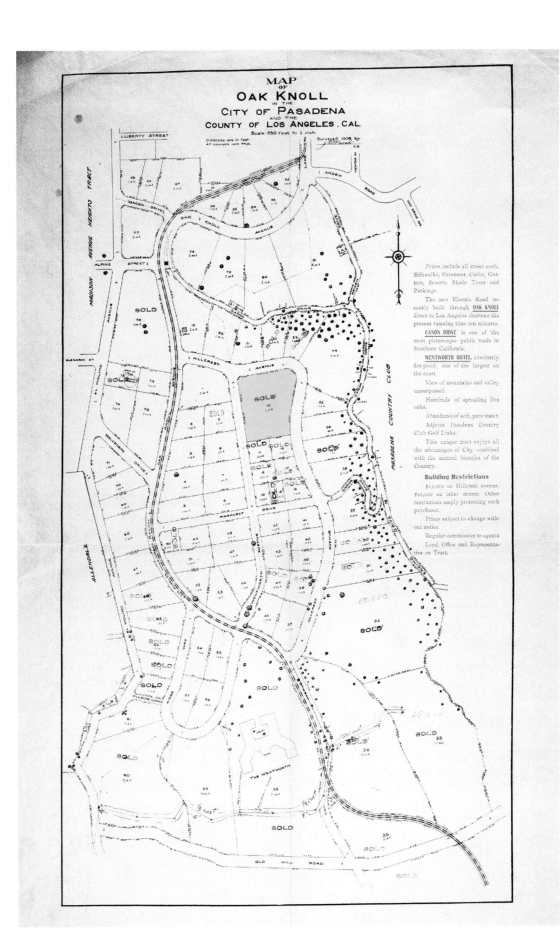

In 1905, real estate developer William R. Staats joined with Henry E. Huntington and A. Kingsley Macomber to offer distinctive properties identified as "Oak Knoll." Huntington's property was adjacent to the Oak Knoll land, as was the property for the Wentworth Hotel (later the Huntington Hotel). The Oak Knoll subdivision design followed the beautiful serpentine street configuration of the plans proposed in 1886, though there were some incidental changes in the size and shape of lots and the street names. The official subdivision survey and promotional map is dated 1906, though the subdivision was not advertised until the end of that year. Blacker's purchase of the 5.1-acre Lot No. 10, at the entrance to the center island of the subdivision, came well before the official survey and may account for the combining of six parcels prior to finalizing the new subdivision. In the same issue of *Maryland Life* that announced the Blackers' first visit of the season, the following advertisement was published: "Oak Knoll will soon make its initial bow to the public. The finishing work to this magnificent property is being rushed through, consistent with our determination to put in only the best of everything."

Oak Knoll Tract Map, 1905.

The Blackers purchased the Oak Knoll property during their 1905–6 winter visit, and engaged Myron Hunt and Elmer Grey to design their house early in 1906. This design was published in the October 1906 issue of *Architectural Record* as "Residence for R. R. Blacker." The selection of Hunt and Grey as architects was very likely associated with Hunt's being the architect for the new pergola and bungalows under construction at the Maryland Hotel while the Blackers were in residence.

Since the Blacker sewer permit for connection to Lot 10 was issued on 19 October 1906, it is clear that Blacker was indeed closely involved with the developers of the Oak Knoll subdivision and may well have been able to affect the actual redesign of land parcels. The 1907 New Year's Day Tournament of Roses Edition of the local newspaper devoted a major story to extol the virtues of Oak Knoll as follows:

By rare good fortune this magnificent property within a few minutes ride from the business center, has been reserved until lately in an undivided tract. It is plentifully dotted with noble live oaks, some of them the growth of two full centuries. There are many knolls or gentle slopes that lend themselves naturally to landscape treatment that retains all of their natural charm. Oak Knoll is the delight of landscape architects and gardeners, and seldom are they afforded such an opportunity by natural characteristics of the land they have to treat. The slopes and ravines, the grand old trees and rare shrubbery from the old ranch place make these home sites most attractive to everyone who has in view the beautification of grounds. . . . All the streets meander in graceful curves and give dignified approach to the building sites consisting of one to five acres. Winding avenues rise to the crest of gentle hills or follow some pretty downward slope leading to wooded shades so as to bring into view each point of variable and surprise the eye with vistas of slopes beyond, of wide stretching valley just below and of the serried mountain range above in sharp contrast of rugged grandeur. . . . Even before Oak Knoll can be said to have really been placed upon the market, about $400,000 worth of property has been sold therein. . . . That most elegant hostelry, the Wentworth, now nearing completion, is in Oak Knoll, being at the very brow in the mesa where the table land drops to the lower valley. Just to the east, Mr. H. E. Huntington, his son, Howard Huntington, and his son-in-law, Gilbert E. Perkins, reserved three building sites comprising about thirty five acres in all. . . . Mr. R. R. Blacker, a wealthy easterner, has secured five acres for a residence in the Italian Villa order, and is preparing now to put into execution his plans for a very elaborate home.

A year later the same New Year's edition would state that Mr. R. R. Blacker had built a palatial Italian villa, costing over $100,000, when in fact the Blacker House was only half constructed and was anything but a palatial Italian villa. On completion of construction, however, the panoramic view across the garden lake to the Blacker House became a principal photograph used in the William R. Staats Co. promotional advertising. From its very beginning, the Blacker House, by its design, its gardens, and its location in the Oak Knoll, has been the flagship of the subdivision, helping to establish the character of the area and by its presence impacting the values of the neighborhood.

Myron Hunt and Elmer Grey

Because of his wife's health, Myron Hunt had come to Pasadena in 1903 from a lucrative architectural practice in Chicago and built his own home on North Grand Avenue, just around the corner from the home and studio of Charles Greene. Elmer Grey had left Milwaukee for the climate of California, later joining Hunt and residing in Pasadena. Grey bypassed a college education, becoming highly skilled as a designer and delineator while apprenticing with Milwaukee architectural firms.

Myron Hunt had attended the School of Architecture at the Massachusetts Institute of Technology between 1890 and 1893, overlapping Charles and Henry Greene's years there by one year, and at the time the Greenes were apprenticing in architectural offices, greatly influenced by architect Henry Hobson Richardson. Henry Greene apprenticed with Shepley, Rutan & Coolidge, the successor firm of the Richardson office. While completing Richardson's work in Chicago and carrying on their own new work for the Chicago Public Library and the Chicago Art Institute, the Shepley, Rutan & Coolidge firm opened their own Chicago branch office in the early 1890s. At the same time and under the direction of Charles Coolidge, the firm began work on the California campus for Stanford University, one of the major commissions on which Henry Greene worked while with the firm in Boston. In 1896, Hunt worked in the Chicago offices of Shepley, Rutan & Coolidge, and the Stanford project caused him to visit these buildings when commencing his own work in 1908 for the Throop Polytechnic Institute (now Cal Tech) in Pasadena. Richardson's friendship and respect for the design principles of landscape architect Frederick Law Olmsted were shared by Coolidge, who carried them into the Stanford design. Olmsted's principles had also served as the inspiration for the natural configuration of the Oak Knoll subdivision, a fact that could not have escaped the attention of Henry Greene when he and Charles were developing their design for the Blacker property.

Myron Hunt's own house in Evanston, Illinois, north of Chicago, and his house built immediately on his arrival in Pasadena in 1903, show the considerable influence of Richardson and the Shingle Style though this aesthetic did not translate into the Hunt and Grey design for the Blackers. Hunt had an interest in gardens, as was discussed in the 29 December 1903 issue of the *Los Angeles Express* in which he had stated that the design of gardens was his favorite occupation. One of Hunt's first commissions on arriving in Pasadena was a garden and pergola for the Maryland Hotel. So successful was it that he was given the commission to do a series of bungalows behind and connecting to the Maryland.

Though both Hunt and Blacker were members of the Chicago Athletic Club and could well have known each other between 1901 and Hunt's departure from Chicago in 1903, it is more likely that Blacker first became aware of Hunt's activities in and around Pasadena and the Maryland Hotel. With Blacker's, Hunt's, and Huntington's connections through the Maryland, their

mutual ties to the Oak Knoll development resulted in Hunt's initial design for the Blackers and Hunt's subsequent house designs for members of the Huntington family.

While Robert and Nellie Blacker actively pursued their community interests, they were not pretentious. They had purchased a large, central, beautiful site in the heart of the newly developed Oak Knoll neighborhood, and likely envisioned a house and garden design responsive to the naturally rolling site with a structure possessing a quiet dignity.

Robert and Nellie Blacker had each had experience with progressive architects in Manistee. Though Manistee had a small population, it had a high ratio of first-class residential architecture, most of it by prominent Chicago architects. Blacker was aware of progressive design philosophies, having been surrounded by examples both in Manistee and Chicago. He had, himself, hired the distinguished Chicago architectural firm of Holabird & Roche for the design of his stable in Manistee.

The Blacker House, Pasadena

The first documented information relating to the design of the Blacker House in Pasadena is the publication of a rendering of the house and garden appearing in the October 1906 issue of *Architectural Record* as a portion of an article entitled "Some Houses by Myron Hunt and Elmer Grey," by Hubert Croly. In the article much is made of the fact that there was less attention paid to gardens and expansive grounds surrounding the house. He states:

Moreover, wonderful as are the opportunities which the soil and climate of southern California offer for landscape gardening, its inhabitants have not yet come to appreciate the value of a careful arrangement and planting of the grounds so as to enhance or to complete an architectural effect. It is the distinction of Messrs. Hunt and Grey that they have consistently used their influence in favor of a high standard of design in this respect and recently have been much more successful in persuading their clients to spend a certain amount of money in the formal treatment of the grounds immediately adjoining their houses.

The article also includes a few paragraphs about the design of the buildings:

The work of Messrs. Hunt and Grey during the years of their practice in Chicago and Milwaukee belonged to what must be called the freer, more picturesque and less formal type of design. It was the result of an attempt to break away from traditional forms and to give their houses an individual and local character. By neither of them, however, was this attempt carried to an extreme. They did not, like certain other architects in the Middle West, seek to ignore and defy the traditions of domestic architecture which have been handed over to us by Europe; they merely sought to modify them so as to make them more appropriate to American conditions and materials, and they succeeded admirably in this effect. Mr. Hunt's houses were bold, definite, coherent pieces of design, composed of comparatively few elements, all of which counted in the most decisive and emphatic way; while the best of Mr. Grey's dwellings were among the most charming of their kind designed by an American Architect.

Many of these same descriptions in the article are more accurately reflective of the work of Greene & Greene. They, too, broke away from traditional forms and drew their inspiration from decidedly regional conditions and materials. Certainly the Blacker 5.1 acres in the center of the rolling terrain of Oak Knoll would offer to Hunt and Grey the opportunities that, according to Croly, they so desired. He went on to say:

Every one of these houses is planned in relation to a spacious formal garden, and it is inevitable that this fact should have a certain influence upon the design of the houses. It cannot be said that these houses will be classic in feeling or that they reproduce any more definitely some traditional domestic style.

Such are the beliefs of the writer, who had written his story from the illustration provided to the magazine, a richly foliated rear view of the Blacker property showing a panorama of the site.

However, the Hunt and Grey design for the Blacker estate has done none of this. The house is indeed incidental in the rendering, is at the center of the site, and has been rendered as though the property were entirely flat. Even the peripheral walls are developed as though for a flat site. Yet, here, where the property provided sloping terrain, there is no attempt by Hunt and Grey to identify with the natural, virgin landscape. The fact that the house is so incidental to the design and lacking of character, as though it were a farmhouse, may well have surprised the Blackers when first presented with the sketch for approval. It did not have the appeal described in the *Architectural Record* article. It said nothing of the conditions nor of the materials of southern California.

Blacker's own life could have inspired the selection of materials. His background in brick and timber was not to be found in the Hunt and Grey design. It is a bit of a surprise that, in the interview that must have occurred between Hunt and Blacker, Blacker's building-materials background did not inspire Hunt to incorporate brick and timber.

What appears to be more logical is that the Hunt and Grey rendering did not seem to convey the kind of house Robert believed appropriate for his wife Nellie. While he was a man of considerable means of his own, Nellie had inherited a yet larger fortune from her father. Perhaps equally important was Robert's experience in the lumber and brick industry throughout his professional life.

The lack of character in the house design may well lie at the core of the Blackers' later rejection of Hunt and Grey as their architects. The *Architectural Record,* on its first page, points out what may have been another factor. The article goes on at some length concerning the higher architectural fees charged by Hunt and Grey and further states that:

Rendering of the Blacker House, as designed by architects Hunt & Grey and published in the October 1906 issue of Architectural Record.

RESIDENCE AND GARDEN FOR MR. R. R. BLACKER.

Pasadena, Cal.   Myron Hunt and Elmer Grey, Architects.

1. Though Hunt and Grey continued to exhibit the Blacker design in the New York Architectural Club exhibition in November 1907, and the drawings were again published in the October 1907 issue of *The Craftsman,* the Blacker name was deleted from the drawings in both instances.

The best possible way to make people understand the value of something is to make them pay for it, and the ability of Messrs. Hunt and Grey to build up a large practice in spite of their higher charges was beneficial to the cause of good architecture in Los Angeles as it was to the welfare of the gentlemen themselves.

Blacker could easily have read these comments or heard about them in the community, and could have felt that he was being charged fees above and beyond those of most other architects. The dismissal of an architect is rare, especially after a commission has been published. As such, the Blackers must have been very disappointed with Hunt and Grey to have taken such a decisive step. Blacker was a very good businessman and would not have taken such an important decision lightly.

The Change of Architects

The precise reason for the Blackers' switch of architects will never be known. Legend also relates that, following the 18 April 1906 San Francisco earthquake, Robert Blacker sat down with Myron Hunt to discuss the design of foundations and their ability to withstand such a natural disaster. Unsatisfied with Hunt's responses, Blacker dismissed him as his architect.

For the plan and rendering of the Hunt and Grey design to be published in the October 1906 *Architectural Record,*[1] the illustrations would have been needed by the publisher as early as June of that year. Since the Blackers arrived for their first visit subsequent to the prior season at the Maryland Hotel around mid-November, and the Greene & Greene survey site drawing of their design is dated November 1906, then the Hunt and Grey design had to have been completed before the Blackers' departure from Pasadena the prior spring. Thus, the Hunt and Grey design meetings with the Blackers and the development and presentation of the plan and rendering must date to the spring of 1906 and the Greene & Greene commission must have been awarded before the Blackers left for Chicago.

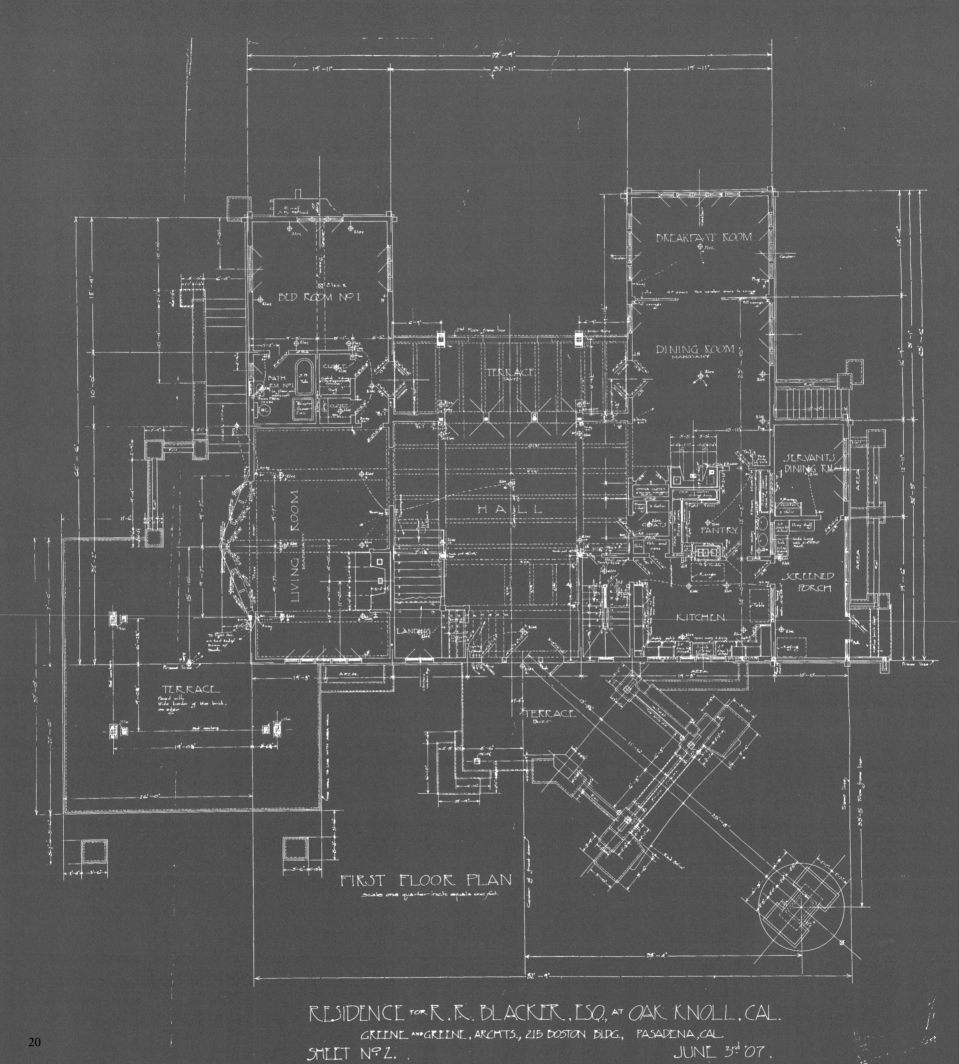

FIRST FLOOR PLAN
Scale one quarter inch equals one foot.

RESIDENCE for R. R. BLACKER, ESQ., at OAK KNOLL, CAL.
GREENE and GREENE, ARCHTS., 215 BOSTON BLDG., PASADENA, CAL.
SHEET Nº 2.   JUNE 3rd '07.

20

2

THE CONSTRUCTION OF A LANDMARK

Left: Greene & Greene first-floor plan, Blacker House.

Right: Blacker House under construction, as published in the October 1948 issue of The Architectural Forum.

The Robert R. Blacker House, Greene & Greene Job No. 209, is dated 7 March 1907 on the base set of working drawings, though early phases of the construction began as much as four months earlier.

In the latter part of 1906, the Oak Knoll Development Company was still in the process of completing the sewer mains in the streets. On 19 October 1906, the Blacker Sewer Permit No. 7069 was issued for the connection to the property line. This was the same month as the *Architectural Record* publication of Myron Hunt's (rejected) design for the Blacker House. The sewer permit and the announcement in *Maryland Life* dated 15 November 1906 that "Mr. And Mrs. R. R. Blacker of Chicago arrive within the next few days for their first visit of this season" suggest that the Blackers had purchased Lot No. 10 in the Oak Knoll tract no later than the spring of 1906. The *Maryland Life* article continued: "It is the Blackers' intention to spend as much of this winter at the Maryland as Mr. Blacker's extensive business interests will admit of."

The "Time Book" kept by W. I. Ott, foreman for the rough construction work on the Blacker property, lists the first week of work ending on 16 February 1907. The following week there were eleven men on the job, including Foreman Ott, two sewer men, and eight laborers. The next week there were two mortar men, and soon a mason—all involved in sewer work. By the end of March, a carpenter was added to the crew, and in early April there were twenty-two carpenters.

Activities on the working drawings were moving swiftly in the Greene offices. Following the initial drawings for the main house, the drawings for the "Outhouses," as they were identified by the Greenes, are dated 16 March 1907 for the keeper's house and garage, Job No. 207, and 27 March 1907 for the lathhouse, also Job No. 207. Additional sheets of detail drawings continued to arrive throughout the entire length of the job.

Since the Ott Time Book continues until the completion of the rough construction work the week of 16 December 1907, it is presumed that Ott was the foreman for the general contractor,

Dawson and Daniels, whose Building Permit No. 5223 for the rough construction in the amount of $30,000 was not issued until 16 April 1907, two months after the sewer work began. That permit covered "a two-story 12 room residence, Dawson and Daniels, Contr., Greene & Greene, Architects, $30,000 and 1 story 4 room keeper's house and garage." There was no mention of the lathhouse. The following day, the *Pasadena Star News* published the permit information clarifying that Dawson and Daniels had the contract for the framing and exteriors only. This is an important clarification as it makes clear that there was no dissatisfaction with Dawson and Daniels' work at the time of the Peter Hall contract and permit for the interiors on 20 April 1908. The dates do raise the question as to what work was being done between 14 December 1907 and 20 April 1908.

The spring of 1908 was a busy time for the architects, the contractors, and the Blackers. Greene & Greene were completing the linen drawings for the large Freeman Ford project; they were in construction on the Gamble House on Westmoreland Place; they presented first sketches for the Charles M. Pratt House in Ojai, California; and they were getting ready to begin the Thorsen project. Work on the Blacker structures was in process, and Robert Blacker, in residence at the Hotel Maryland in the heart of Pasadena, continued his activities with the Manistee Safety Deposit Company, the A. H. Lyman Co. Wholesale and Retail Drugs and Stationary, the Manistee & Grand Rapids Railroad Co., and the Chicago–South Haven shipping line in Chicago, among other interests, and continued to maintain his ownership and address at the house he had built in Manistee, Michigan.

21

Throughout 1907, the Blacker House appeared in both local and national publications. The *Pasadena News* headline "Palatial Oak Knoll Home" claimed that the house would incorporate novel improvements and the structure promised to be "one of the handsomest in the Beautiful Crown City." The article included important information that Blacker purchased the property many months earlier and intended to complete the billiard room in the basement later, clarifying that its construction in 1910 was not an afterthought.

The main house was not the first of the several structures to be completed on the Blacker property. While it, the garage, keeper's house, and the lathhouse were all begun at the same time, the time of their completions varied widely. The 9 November 1907 *Pasadena Star Evening* published the following:

As a pleasant surprise to Mr. And Mrs. R. R. Blacker when they arrived at the Maryland yesterday, after spending the summer in the east, their rooms at Hotel Maryland were decorated with beautiful flowers from their own gardens at Oak Knoll. The Blacker residence at Oak Knoll is nearing completion and the capitalist expects to occupy it inside of two or three weeks.

The reader may presume, mistakenly, that the article was referring to the main house when, in fact, rough framing was far from being completed. Its full basement took as long to rise above ground as it took to complete the garage, the keeper's house, and the lathhouse. What the newspaper article failed to tell us was that the Blackers took temporary residence in the keeper's house around the beginning of December 1907.

The construction progress is confirmed by Charles Greene's own photographs of the Blacker work. In all of his images taken on a single day, the garage, keeper's house, and lathhouse were just being completed: ladders remained in position for final detail work, and the general area was typical of a construction site, including stacks of lumber, equipment, and sheds. Alongside the keeper's house and the lathhouse can be seen several planting beds being carefully watered by a temporary sprinkling system. In his most important image, which includes Charles's hat in the lower left corner of the photo, the main Blacker House was framed only on the first floor. The second-floor wall framing had yet to begin to rise and the wood sheathing was just beginning to be applied on the southwest corner of the dining room.

Blacker House under construction, from Charles Greene's negative.

The Outbuildings

Greene & Greene were quick to seize the opportunity to please a new and wealthy client and completed the drawings for the three major accessory buildings as well as the main house in a very short time. All these buildings were lined up nearer Wentworth than the main house and evenly spaced to the south. The longitudinal axis of each outbuilding was on the east-west line; thus, all faced north.

Garage

The northernmost of the three is the garage. It was a two-story rectangular structure with five-foot gable overhangs. The roof had a raised central section that overlapped the lower roof a full five feet to each side of the lower section. The raised roof created a clerestory all around. The ridge of the upper and lower roofs had a five-inch rise at the ends, which softened the roofline and assisted drainage. The first-floor level was divided nearly in half by the stairway and toilet room, with a two-car garage on the west and a room for storage on the east. The second floor had two bedrooms above the garage and an unfinished loft above the storage room. Each bedroom was accompanied by a large walk-in closet. The garage doors were massive and expressed their composite members, as did those in the main house. Thick strap hinges held the garage doors in place. The garage was clearly for automobiles and not for horses. There was even a mechanic's pit to help service the cars. As with the main house, the garage was sheathed in green-stained split shakes with eleven inches exposed. Both ends of the building were fitted with vertical trellises, and a pergola beginning above the south storage-room door connected it to the keeper's house. Similar braced supports as were used in the porte cochere held it in position. Because there was no chimney, the garage had a spare, clean look.

Greene & Greene drawing for the Blacker garage.

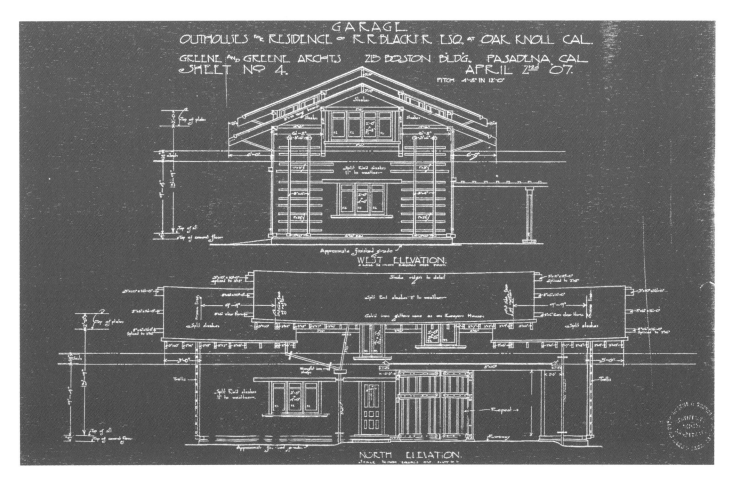

Keeper's House

The keeper's house was the residence for the groundskeeper. It was set a bit farther west than the garage and was connected to it by the pergola. The single story held two bedrooms, a living room, dining room, kitchen with pantry, and a bathroom. (The keeper's house has been altered and added to several times since Mrs. Blacker's passing.) Off the kitchen bay, a large shed overhang kept out the low morning sun. A living room fireplace extended through the roof and was finished the same as those in the main house. There was a crawl space under the house, ventilated at several locations around the perimeter brick foundation.

Lathhouse

The lathhouse was much like the familiar greenhouse, except it had no glass, just long strips of lath to provide shade for more-delicate flowers. It, too, had an east-west ridgeline. The ridgeline was flat, not upturned as the other two outhouses, as it did not need to deal with water drainage. The lath stopped short of the rafter ends and allowed them to pass in a now-familiar Greene & Greene fashion. The building was a simple braced frame set upon a half-lapped mud sill. Angle braces strengthened each corner.

The Blacker House in Context

In December 1907, Robert Blacker further established himself in Pasadena. He became a partner in the Vista Del Arroyo Hotel. On 27 December 1907 the *Pasadena News* ran the following story:

Vista Del Arroyo Has Incorporated: Vista Del Arroyo, the hotel on South Grand Avenue which celebrated its twenty-fifth anniversary Christmas day, has incorporated for $50,000., R. R. Blacker, J. M. Fowler and H. I. Steward being named as incorporators. The Crown City Investment Company, which owned one-half of the property, has sold its half to R. R. Blacker of Chicago, H. M. Fowler retaining his half.

Left to right: Southwest view of Blacker garage, keeper's house, and lathhouse.

Though the estimated cost for the rough construction and exterior work for the main house was $30,000, according to the permits, and on 22 April 1908 Peter Hall's Permit No. 6287 for the woodwork of the interiors of the main house only was in the amount of $20,000, the *Pasadena Star* ran a story that the residence was going to cost $70,000. Notations in the Greene & Greene records break down the costs for Mr. Robert R. Blacker projects as follows:

Main house, furniture, fixtures, and grounds	$70,925.00
Keeper's house and garage total	5,771.00
Pergola (1910)	1,321.00
Billiard room (1910)	3,650.00
Furniture (partial in 1912)	544.00
Additions to sleeping porch (1914)	1,019.00

Keeper's house and garage, from the southeast. All photographs by Charles Greene.

Main hall and stairway.

All the interior woodworking to complete the rough frame of the main house for occupancy was finished by Peter Hall's master craftsmen in five months. The Notice of Completion was filed with the City of Pasadena and reported in the *Pasadena News* on 9 September 1908. Work on the Blacker estate was, however, far from complete, and the close working relationship between Robert and Nellie Blacker and Charles and Henry Greene would continue for many years to come.

In addition to the ongoing projects at the Blacker estate, the design and construction of the William R. Thorsen House in Berkeley and the Annie Blacker House in Pasadena were so closely intertwined with the Blackers and the Greenes, it is essential that these projects be discussed in the context of the continuing work on the Oak Knoll site.

The Thorsen House
In October of 1908, Charles Greene traveled to Berkeley to confer with Mrs. Blacker's sister, Carrie, and her husband, William R. Thorsen, regarding the design of what would be the last of the Greenes' ultimate wood commissions. A month later, in November of 1908, the Thorsens visited with the Blackers while in town to meet with the Greenes to review a second scheme for their home drawn up by Henry Greene.

The progressive architectural interests among the Blacker, Canfield, and Thorsen families was remarkable. William R. Thorsen's grandfather had been a noted architect in Christiansand, Norway. Thorsen and Canfield had turned the commissions for their large Manistee residences over to William Le Baron Jenny, distinguished for his progressive design for the Chicago Home Insurance Building, the first steel-frame structure in the United States.[1] Thorsen, like Blacker and Charles Canfield, had left Manistee near the turn of the century when the tax structures changed and the forests played out, finally settling in northern California. Caroline Thorsen frequently looked up to her brother-in-law Robert Blacker and followed his lead in the selection of Greene & Greene as architects for the Thorsen House in Berkeley.

1. Architect William Le Baron Jenny, 1832–1907, was educated at the Ecolé de Beaux Arts in Paris, began architectural practice in Chicago in 1868, and trained many young architects, including Martin Roche and William Holabird, all instrumental in the development of the Chicago skyscraper.

On 10 April 1909, the building permits were pulled for the Thorsen House, Greene & Greene Job No. 230, in Berkeley, California.

The Thorsens' site differed substantially from the Blackers', and its tight corner lot was considerably smaller than the vast open acreage of the Blacker estate. The Thorsens' property sloped dramatically up from its west-facing frontage and was bounded on the north by the steep grade of the side street. Because of the busy traffic at the intersection and the small amount of land, the Greenes positioned the house along the two street frontages, creating a buffer to the noise and embracing an internal rear yard for a modest garden. The Thorsen design is somewhat unique due to the varying grades and levels of the grounds, terraces, and interiors. To some, this polished, southern California Shingle Style Craftsman house in the foothills of Berkeley was vastly different from the eclectic traditions and rustic creations then prevalent in the Berkeley hills, where the exceptional works of Bernard Maybeck, Julia Morgan, and Louis Mullgardt, among others, were establishing their own presence. Like the Blacker House, the Thorsen House was furnished with Greene & Greene furniture and lighting fixtures, though to a much lesser degree.

William R. and Caroline Canfield Thorsen House, Berkeley, California, 1909; Greene & Greene, architects.

27

Their personal residence was not the only construction work going on for Robert and Nellie Blacker. In January of 1909, they funded the construction for the first cottages of the La Vina Tuberculosis Sanitorium in the foothills of Altadena, just north of Pasadena. This was just the beginning of many community projects the Blackers would support during their years in Pasadena.

At the Blacker site, after the completion of the main house, additions and alterations were continuing to be designed and built. In 1910, Greene & Greene Job No. 249, the freestanding pergola in the garden by the lake, was constructed at a cost of $1,321.00, along with Job No. 250, the development of the basement-level billiard room at a cost of $3,650.00.

Inset: The freestanding pergola stood alone in the Blacker garden on the east-west axis of the living room terrace and near the island end of the lake.

Archival photograph of Blacker gardens and lake, looking toward Mount Wilson to the northeast.

29

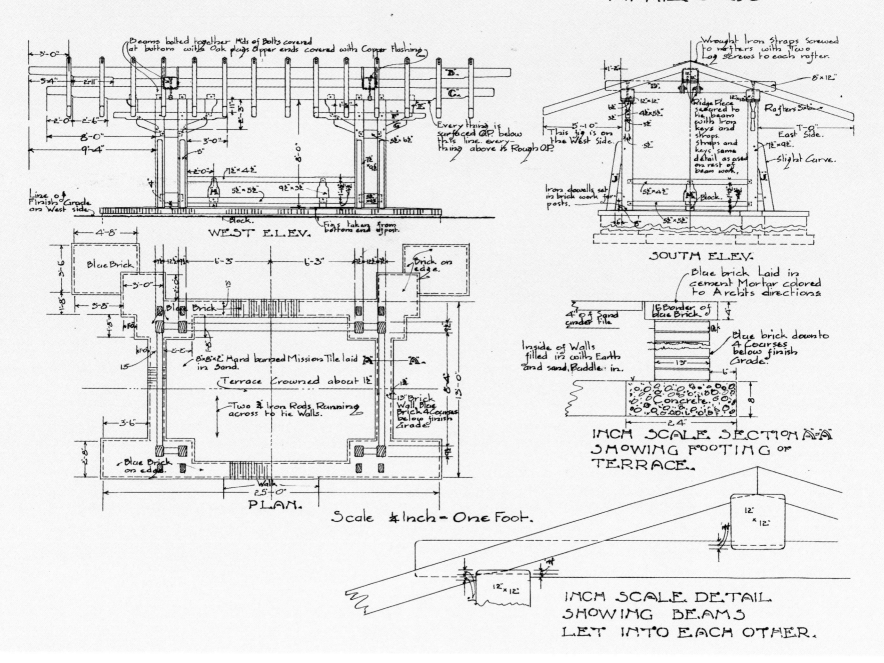

In August of 1910, Greene & Greene Job No. 257 involved the design and working drawings for a cottage in Long Beach, California, for R. R. Blacker, a modest bungalow built at a cost of $1,529.[2] Two years later, Blacker again turned to his architects to design two additional bungalows in Long Beach at a cost of $3,200 for the two, Greene & Greene Job. No. 289.[3] Later, in 1912, more of the Blacker House furniture, Greene & Greene Job No. 291, was completed.

In search of a residence in his own neighborhood for his maiden sisters, Mary and Annie Blacker, Robert first gave serious consideration to the purchase of a recently completed bungalow by Greene & Greene for Dr. S. S. Crow, located around the

corner from his own Oak Knoll residence. The Crow House had been placed on the market due to the death of Dr. Crow's wife. While this was a remarkable house that Henry Greene had designed, Mary and Annie preferred to be nearer their nephew, Edward James Simpson Blacker, Robert Blacker's adopted nephew, who was living a few blocks away on South Madison Avenue. Purchasing a lot directly across the street from Edward, Annie Blacker, following the lead of her older brother, turned to Henry Greene to design a nine-room two-story house, Greene & Greene Job No. 295. With Peter Hall as the general contractor, the house was constructed for $14,075 and the garage, Greene & Greene Job No. 296, for $1,005.

2. No address for this modest cottage has yet been located, though it is likely that this is the same Santa Monica cottage located at 215 Georgina Avenue, where Regina Blacker was living at the time of his death in September 1931.

3. No drawings exist for these bungalows, and their location and status has not been determined to date.

Right: Designed in 1909 by Henry Greene, the Dr. S. S. Crow House was considered by Robert Blacker for his sister Annie Blacker. Her desire to be near her nephew prompted Blacker to instead commission Henry to design the Annie Blacker House on Madison Avenue, several blocks from Robert and Nellie Blacker's home. The Crow House was then purchased in 1911 by Edward S. Crocker, who commissioned additional gardens and structures. Thereafter, the house was identified as the Crow-Crocker House.

Left: Original Greene & Greene drawing for the freestanding garden pergola.

Right: Annie Blacker House, designed in 1909; Greene & Greene, architects; Henry M. Greene, designer.

For the Annie Blacker House, Henry Greene was sensitive to the more modest scale of this neighborhood adjacent to the exclusive Oak Knoll tract. Sympathetic to the other houses along the street, he created a basic two-story bungalow with central hall, a design Henry believed to be efficient and economical, offering the most amenities for the investment. His disciplined and straightforward design ethic is well demonstrated in his composition of the multiple gable roofs and the asymmetrical massing of the front

elevation. Though the decorative arts appeared less frequently in the Annie Blacker House, Henry's designs for the clear-art-glass windows of the dining room and hall cabinets are superb. His careful attention to the hierarchy of proportional relationships of the strong linear composition is enhanced by the softness of the treatment of the leading. Construction on the Annie Blacker House began in April of 1912 and was completed in late October.

The first major alteration of the Blacker House came in 1914, Greene & Greene Job No. 315, following the Blackers' occupancy. At this time the second-level covered balcony off the southwest bedroom was enclosed with clear-glass windows and solid lower walls. It had been originally built open to the breezes as a sheltered outdoor room overlooking the gardens and the San Gabriel Valley.

Second-level balcony, enclosed.

A fountain in the rear courtyard came in 1928, a project that Charles Greene designed in his Carmel studio and had made in San Francisco. The bird fountain was the last Greene & Greene design for the Blackers. Henry, however, continued to oversee the maintenance of the house and grounds following Robert Roe Blacker's death on 16 September 1931 and throughout the years of Mrs. Blacker's residence.

*The Blacker, Thorsen, and Frost
families in the Blacker garden,
8 June 1928. Left to right: Ida
Canfield Frost, E. W. Frost,
Nellie Canfield Blacker,
Caroline Canfield Thorsen,
William R. Thorsen, Robert
Roe Blacker.*

In a letter of 4 February 1942 to Charles, Henry wrote:

*I called on Mrs. Blacker and found her feeble but able to be about.
. . . The place looks lovely now with the green lawns and trees and
shrubbery; vistas, bird bath and pool. The inside of the house is
perfect yet; apparently not a scar or shrinkage or blemish. Quite a
number of years ago I had Savage go over all of the woodwork and
furniture; and so it looks and is as smooth as velvet as yet. . . .*

*Overleaf: South elevation from the
present rear gardens.*

34

The Greene & Greene design for the Blacker Pasadena house differed from the Hunt and Grey design in a number of important and specific ways. Their design thinking acknowledged a new and modern age, including the advent of the automobile and its impact on the development of land planning. They developed the site in sympathy with the natural topography, the gardens responding to and enhancing the natural lake on the site. They positioned the house in the corner of the property. They gave greater attention to the exterior terraces. They added a motor court with a dramatic entrance porte cochere. They carried out the design in an entirely different twentieth-century building vocabulary, one that drew its inspiration from the background of its clients, the character of the land, and the culture of southern California. All of these things were expressed in the Greenes' new and fully refined personal architectural style.

The Site Development

Charles and Henry Greene had strongly disagreed with Hunt and Grey on the siting of the house at the center of the property and with their plan to level the naturally sloping terrain. Greene & Greene positioned the main house to the northwest corner of the site, near the entrance to the Oak Knoll neighborhood, and created a separate circular-entry motor court and swung the drive down the west side of the house to the garage, where it exited directly to Wentworth Avenue. Behind the garage, a keeper's house and lathhouse completed the needs of the Blackers' new estate.

Archival photograph showing rear and side elevations prior to the 1912 addition of the pergola off the dining room, lower left, and the 1914 enclosure of the balcony, upper left.

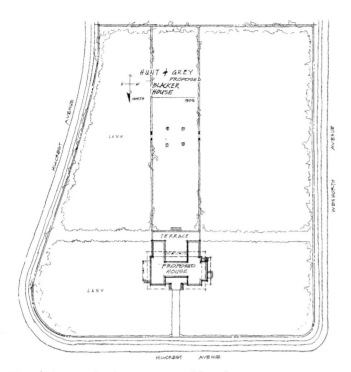

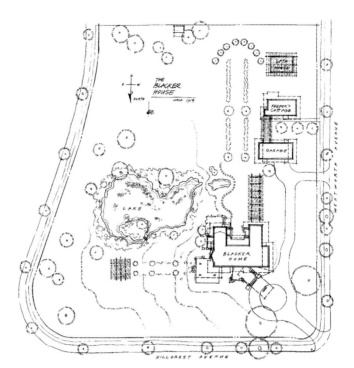

Hunt & Grey site-plan drawing interpreted from the rendering published in the October 1906 issue of The Architectural Record.

Greene & Greene site-plan drawing reconstructed from archival photographs.

The *Los Angeles Times* story on 10 May 1908, written when the construction of the house was not complete, provides an important image of the grounds and landscape as it was originally designed by the Greenes.

. . . An artificial lake to the south, with a miniature mountain brooklet, running with a musical tinkle over a series of rapids of rock and fallen trees. The water passes through a series of small rock walled pools, in which various varieties of goldfish sport, and finally reaches the large basin, where the images of the house, and surrounding buildings are reflected.

This newspaper description becomes more vivid when viewed with the few Leroy Hulbert panoramic photographs taken from the southwest and from the southeast, which portray the Greenes' desire to draw the landscape from the natural terrain of the original Oak Knoll Ranch property. It is precisely this response to the natural site that distinguishes the Greenes' design from the Hunt and Grey design. By adjusting the existing natural swales of the site, they enhanced the lake, defined its edge with smooth granite boulders from the nearby arroyo, and took advantage of the irregular site to join interiors and garden from both the main floor and the basement level. Full-grown palm trees in eight-foot-wide wooden containers were drawn to the site by a team of ten horses and carefully placed into the Greenes' landscape design.

The geometry of the site and the essence of its landscape layout emanated from the heart of the house on two cross axes. The north-south line through the entry hall carried the eye through the rear courtyard to the cutting gardens and the south limit of the property. This strong axis defined the differences between the order of the house and the irregular sloping terrain at the edge of the lake. Along the axis, off the dining room wing of the house, the garage, keeper's house, and lathhouse continued the parallel line of structures along Wentworth Avenue. On the east side of this axis, the site was allowed to roll naturally to the gentle curve of Hillcrest Avenue, which defined the northern and eastern borders of the property. Greene & Greene purposefully paid careful attention to the topography of the land and allowed it to direct and inspire their own design.

A strong east-west axis off the living-room terrace paralleled the front of the house and was defined by two rows of tubbed palm trees that led through open, rolling lawn to the timbered pergola near the lake. Vines climbed over the open rafters of the pergola, providing respite from the warmth of the day, a place for quiet reading, or a spot for entertaining guests at tea. From here, as well as from the various terraces and balconies, one could view the San Gabriel Mountains to the north or the San Gabriel Valley and the ravine to the east.

Hunt & Grey plan of first floor.

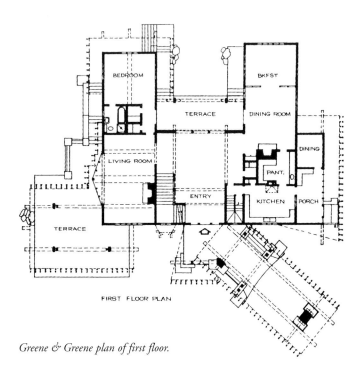

Greene & Greene plan of first floor.

The Plans

The floor plan of the Blacker House was the design of Myron Hunt and Elmer Grey. A careful study of their plan published in the October 1907 issue of *The Craftsman* differs only slightly from the final Greene & Greene plan. The Greenes' plan relocated the servants'-quarters stairway, substantially enlarged the entry hall, added an angled bay to the living room, expanded the front and side terraces, and added a long porte cochere to the northwest of the entry door.

The Greenes developed and brought forward the full thrust of their new and highly refined timber style to create what became the largest and most elaborate of their wooden masterworks. Here they demonstrated the fundamental concepts of their Arts & Crafts philosophy: the provision of shade and shelter in a hot arid climate, free cross-circulation of air, and an open relationship between house and garden. This applied equally well to the large estate and to the modest bungalow, as manifested by the compatibility of the scale of the main Blacker House with the three outbuildings. To break further from the formality of the Hunt and Grey plan, the Greenes designed a long timbered porte cochere that angled from the central entry and was supported by a massive clinker-brick pier in the island of the grand circular drive.

The differences in the two designs are noted in two important articles written early and late in the construction of the Blacker House. Drawing upon the Hunt and Grey rendering in the October 1906 issue of *Architectural Record,* the 1 January 1907 issue of the *Pasadena Daily News* reported that:

Mr. R. R. Blacker, wealthy easterner, has secured five acres for a residence on the Italian Villa order, and is preparing now to put into execution his plans for a very elaborate home.

Inaccurate as is this report, it demonstrates dramatically the differences between the Hunt and Grey and the Greene & Greene designs. Partway through the construction, on 10 May 1908, a lengthy story in the *Los Angeles Times* written prior to the completion of the interiors ascribes the Blacker House design differently as:

. . . of a modified Swiss architecture, with characteristics of the modern California bungalow apparent in many places, the building fits well into the general surroundings of oak trees, spreading lawns, and winding drives, with a background of foothills and mountains.

Stairway to east terrace from rear garden.

The Structure

To Greene & Greene it was important that the fundamental nature of the structure and the materials be honestly expressed on both the exterior and interior. The feature that had impressed the brothers in the design of the Japanese Pavilion at the Chicago World Columbian Exposition in 1893 was the straightforward expression of the component parts of the structure—the posts, beams, rafters, and skin (the wall panels)—used frankly. The inherent qualities of each part of the construction brought to the design its own appropriate color, texture, and rhythm.

Detail of metal-strap and wedge joinery connecting the post-and-beam structure with the open-timber truss.

The careful attention to scale and proportion in the composition of these essential components made any kind of applied artificial decoration unnecessary.

The Blacker exterior states exactly what it is: a wood-timber structure in southern California, as fresh and forthright as a Japanese temple, as shingle-clad as the New England Shingle Style, and as lyrical in its massing and fenestration as the chalets of the Black Forest or the Swiss Alps. And while it is all of these in spirit, it is none of these in reality, for the Greenes infused each new project with distinct regional considerations, looking first to climate, environment, materials available, and the habits and tastes of the owner as the initial determinants of their designs.

The Exterior

Built upon rugged clinker-brick foundations and broad terra-cotta-paved terraces, the powerful post-and-beam structure, with its brazen exploitation of metal-strap and wooden-dowel joinery, broad roof overhangs, projecting outriggers and rafter tails, provides a constant ballet of silhouettes and shadows as the sun moves through the day. Within the strong and orderly design is a structural system with the opportunity for variation, which, under the Greenes' firm control, allowed them to infuse their designs with a relaxed flexibility. So they pushed, pulled, tucked or turned the composition when called upon to do so, without sacrificing either structural integrity or visual continuity.

The east-facing living room terrace overlooked the lake and garden pergola of the 5.1-acre site prior to the land subdivision in 1948 following Mrs. Blacker's death.

The angled east wall of the living room invites transition to the east terrace, carried out in terra-cotta pavers.

"Structurally it is a blessing: . . . in this sort of thing there is only an honesty that is sometimes almost brazen. It is a wooden style built woodenly. . . ." [1]

1. Ralph Adams Cram,
   *American Country
   Houses of Today* (New
   York: Architectural Book
   Publishing Co., 1913).

43

Left: East terrace transition to the gardens.

Right: The massive timbered porte cochere struck out at an angle to the house, allowing an unobstructed view from the living room.

By using color as a further differentiation between components, the architects brought to the composition another level of richness. Structural timbers, rafters, and window trim were stained a medium dark brown; the redwood shakes of the exterior walls were green; and windows and doors were left a light natural finish. Combined with the rich red-brown tones of the clinker-brick foundations, the slate gray-green of the composition rolled roofing, the rust of the metal-strapping details, and the multicolored imagery from the leaded-and-stained-glass windows, the Blacker House presented a lively and varied color palette. The use of Cabot's transparent penetrating-oil stains was a critical factor in the Greene & Greene exterior color specification. The transparency of the stains allowed for the grain of the timbers and the varied coloration of the wood to respond differently to the stains. This was especially effective on the split redwood shakes, where not only did the shakes differ in texture but also in color, resulting in a variation that gave the entire exterior a life and vitality that the flat uniformity of solid body stains and paints cannot duplicate.

The Entry Porch

To enter the Blacker House is to be subjected to a range of impressions. From the circular drive covered by the timber-trussed porte cochere, the visitor ascends the broad brick stairs onto a Mission-tile entry porch that conveys a sense of intimacy with its lower roof and the heavy timber trusses embracing the space. In the evening, broad-hooded lanterns cast a soft glow across the terrace as the visitor follows the angle of the porch toward the tripartite bank of entry doors. Here, as in the Gamble House, the central door is wide and hospitable, and the lack of a screen promises an easy welcome.

Right: View from entrance door through the porte cochere to clinker-brick pier.

Far right: View of entrance doors from under the porte cochere near the drive.

45

The Main Hall

As the visitor steps into the main hall, one is first welcomed by the warmth of the teak wall paneling and the lighting lanterns, and then is greeted by the long vista of the southern garden through the broad bank of clear-glass French doors opening onto the rear courtyard. Overhead, the ceiling is of Douglas fir heavy-timber construction, and between the beams are panels of Port Orford cedar exhibiting a hint of difference between the transparent rubbed stains of the frames and the central panels. Square pegs acknowledge the joinery of their construction and complete the hierarchy of Henry Greene's proportional relationships, which are essential to the grace of Greene & Greene designs. Five hanging lanterns designed for the main hall softly illuminate, whether by day or evening, and despite the somewhat limited technology of the era in which they were created, become magical points of light, casting a warm glow around the space and across the grain of the hand-rubbed interior paneling. Inez Peterson, who worked for the Blackers, recalled that "the wood all through the house is very smooth and satiny. Mr. Blacker usually stopped to rub his hands over it when going from one room to another."

In 1909, when Greene & Greene were designing the house in Berkeley for Nellie Blacker's sister, Caroline Canfield Thorsen, Mrs. J. W. Purchas, sister of William R. Thorsen, visited the just-completed Blacker House and wrote her brother her personal and sometimes humorous observations:

Well I find the outside of the house and grounds very pretty and attractive but my impressions after moving through the various rooms was that the architect has let his fancy run riot in wood. There is so much wood about the outside that when one finds oneself encased in wooden rooms, wood walls, wood ceiling, wood floors, wood furniture, wood fixtures for light—well, one has a little bit the feeling of a spider scrambling from one cigar box to another.

The hall is excelleent—as that is a public room and can take the wood surroundings but my own feeling would run to more warmth of color and softer things. However these are all individual tastes. Only I hope you won't have quite so much wood. . . . I find the porches, the porte cochere, etc., most attractive. . . .

All Mr. Greene's woodwork is a delight for the softness of its finish. It is like fresh butter or paste squeezed out of a tube, so soft are the surfaces and corners. . . .[2]

Main hall two-level column detail.

Main hall with original furniture on

loan from the Los Angeles County

Museum of Art.

2. Courtesy Professor
Robert Judson Clark.

Above: The pointed bay of the living room opens directly to the east terrace.

Left: Archival photograph of the furnished living room.

The Living Room

The Blacker living room was executed in a dark mahogany with wall paneling of ribbon grain, light oak floors, a painted canvas ceiling, and gold-metal-leaf frieze. The pointed bay of French doors leading to the east terrace expands the living room significantly. Spanning the bay, the hand-rubbed timber truss is so deftly handled that it does not overwhelm the delicate detail. Opposite the bay is the broad fireplace, one of four in the house. The room is a rectangle relieved by the bay and the broad portal to the main hall. Dark timbers divide the ceiling and hanging lanterns, open-top art-glass baskets of light that enliven the earth-toned walls and the gold-metal-leaf lily pads of the frieze and ceiling.

To each side of the main hall, the two wings of the plan contain the living room and bedroom no. 1 to the left and the dining room and service rooms to the right. Wide openings connect the dining and living rooms to the main hall, uncluttered by doors or portieres, thus enhancing the feeling of spaciousness and inter-relationships. These two side wings embrace the central courtyard and are entered directly from the rear of the main hall through the French doors. Robert and Nellie Blacker particularly loved the main hall and arranged Charles Greene's couch and armchairs to face the rear court with a view through the cutting gardens, spending considerably more time there than in the living room.

The Dining Rooms

West of the main hall are the dining room and the breakfast room, separated only by a wall of glass doors, which, when removed, allow for the two areas to be opened into one large dining hall. The dining room, like the living room, is paneled in dark mahogany with detail, trim, lighting fixtures, and furniture to match.

The breakfast room projects a little farther south than the east wing, an attempt to capture a broader view of the east gardens and the lake. Although, in the summer, the sun arrives a little after the breakfast hour because of the east-wing shadow, the room is bathed in sunshine throughout the late morning and into the late afternoon. Three iridescent art-glass windows pick up light, adding subtle texture and color above the windows on the three walls. Both dining rooms are highlighted by hanging light trays suspended by elaborate leather straps and wood rings that drop from large, cross-membered, wood ceiling plates.

The Service Rooms

The service area was comprised of the pantry, the kitchen, a screened porch, and a small servants' dining room. In typical Greene fashion, the details of these service rooms are consistent with other rooms in the house, though rendered with differing species of wood. The plaster walls of the pantry and kitchen have scribed tile and are trimmed in Port Orford cedar. Cabinets have been left natural with a hand-rubbed finish. Throughout the service area, the counters are finished in natural pine. The screened porch was carried out in Douglas fir vertical board-and-batten wall paneling and complemented by the tongue-and-groove sheathing of the open-rafter fir ceiling treated with a rubbed natural-oil finish. While the side service door is directly off the screened porch, it is discreetly hidden from the motor court by a wing wall detailed into the main front elevation of the house.

Breakfast room, looking into the dining room.

Left: Axial vista of the courtyard fountain from the main hall looking out to Nellie Blacker's cutting gardens.

Dining room, fireplace and china cabinet.

Restored kitchen, looking into the breakfast porch, originally the screened porch.

Left: Leaded-and-stained-glass bay window at the landing of the main hall stairway.

Main Stair and Upper Hall

The upper hall is connected to the main hall by an elaborately detailed wooden stairway that joins the two levels. Extraordinary care was given to the scale and proportion of its parts and the joinery of its separate elements. From every angle, each new vista offers differing impressions as the light of the day passes.

The upper hall shares the common bay window at the stair landing, offering different perspectives of the stained-glass imagery from the two levels. A bank of casement windows lets in the soft north light throughout the day.

Right: Upper hall.

Left: Panorama of the main hall and the upper hall, viewed from the stair landing.

The Bedrooms

The second level of the Blacker House was devoted to sleeping quarters. All rooms were finished with plaster walls, canvas-covered ceilings, Port Orford wood trim and doors, and a variety of Greene & Greene–designed lighting fixtures.

The master suite occupies the entire east wing and includes bedroom no. 2, an east roof terrace, a dressing room, bathroom no. 2, a sun porch, and a south balcony. The rich café-au-lait walls are trimmed with natural cedar also used to detail the fireplace mantel.

The dressing room relates to the color and decor of the master bedroom and serves as the corridor from the bedroom to the bathroom and the small sunroom beyond. The sunroom is a wood-paneled room with extraordinary finger-lap joinery transitioning to the detail of the frieze and to the heavy timber construction of the ceiling. As a dramatic statement, the Greenes changed the finish of the wood as each element stacked above the other, from smooth-dressed hand-sanded trim pieces to rough-sawn to rough-cut. In the rougher elements, a slight wash gives distinction to those timbers out of reach, a happy expression of the joining of interior and exterior detail in a room that was a bit of both.

Right: Finger-lap wood joinery detail and interior window of the bathroom, viewed from the sunroom adjacent to the dressing room of bedroom no. 2.

In the north end of the west wing, two servants' rooms are accessed through a hidden door in a wall of cabinets at the head of the stairs of the upper hall. The related bathroom no. 4, though smaller, is given the same detail and quality of materials as the balance of the house. A back stairway leads down to the kitchen and service rooms directly below.

Bedroom no. 3, between the east and west wings of the house, was designed for the extra guest. With its two wide doors opened, this bedroom expands and functions as a day room off the upper hall. With its interconnecting hall to bath no. 3, it can also be used as a suite when combined with bedroom no. 4 in the west wing.

Bedroom no. 4 was the primary guest bedroom when needed, and an upstairs family room for the day-to-day living pattern. Tucked in a corner off the upper hall with a large covered balcony, it offered a casual atmosphere for relaxing, reading, and day activities.

The balcony—originally open, with a wood railing, glass windscreens to the sides, and a truss and roof-structure covering of massive timber—was enclosed by the Greenes in 1914 at the request of the Blackers. Apparently this was installed without the full enthusiasm of Charles Greene, for in his detailing of the enclosure, he went out of his way to retain the open wood railing. In so doing, he constructed a thin inner wall to allow the rail to remain, possibly hoping that someday the enclosure would be removed and the sleeping porch reopened. The simplest construction for the enclosure would have been to remove the rail and install a low exterior wall clad in shakes matching the adjacent walls. Charles's design was more difficult to execute and virtually impossible to access for routine maintenance.

The interior of the balcony is thrilling. Its high-roof, open-truss construction is exposed to the space. Built of rough lumber, its rugged nature is therefore most curious as an enclosed interior room, begging to be opened to the breezes again.

Right: Window of bathroom no. 2 as seen from the interior.

Below: Bathroom no. 1 celebrates the experience of the shower.

Interior of balcony as enclosed by Greene & Greene in 1914.

Enclosed balcony exterior exhibits original railing retained by Greene & Greene.

The Bathrooms

The main-floor bathroom no. 1 celebrates the shower. While the double-ringed construction of the shower allows for a curtain, a peripheral shower ring, a central drenching showerhead, temperature controls, and portable nozzle, its most exciting feature is its sheer sculptural delight. It is fun, a conversation piece and a work of art in an otherwise utilitarian room.

In all of the bathrooms of the main two floors, the walls are of a three-by-six-inch white tile laid horizontally. Floors are two-inch-hexagonal white tiles. Freestanding, single-pedestal, oval lavatories and claw-footed tubs in white porcelain complement the interior with a white John Douglas water closet featuring a wood tank and seat.

The guest bathroom no. 1 and the master bathroom no. 2 are detailed in mahogany and Port Orford cedar, respectively. In the remaining bathrooms, the wood trim and detail are painted in a typical Greene & Greene light-putty-cream color.

Bathroom no. 3, with wood trim painted as originally specified by Greene & Greene.

Original stained-glass windows in bathroom no. 1.

The Billiard Room

Although not constructed until 1910, one year after the Blackers had taken occupancy, the billiard room had been a part of the design program from the beginning. Its construction was delayed until later because of the considerable amount of other work that had to be completed before the Blackers could move into the main house. This delay made it possible for the Greenes to allow the air-duct system across the ceiling of the billiard room to generate the concept for their ceiling design.

By responding to the topography of the site, the billiard room opened directly to the exterior grade. Windows to the south and east allowed light and air into the low-ceilinged space, which was large enough to handle the full-sized billiard table at one end as well as Mr. Blacker's game table and wet bar at the other. On the exterior, the clinker-brick foundations for the main floors are expressed at this lower level, making a clear statement of the hierarchy of levels and functions on the exterior elevations of the house.

Above: Basement-level billiard room.

Above left: Wire-brushed redwood detail and wall sconce in the billiard room.

Below: Detailed wood ceiling of the billiard room.

Working with the undulating terrain of the original site, the architects were able to give the
basement-level billiard room direct access to the gardens off the southeast wing of the house.

4

For Charles and Henry Greene, the decorative arts were a natural extension of their architectural design. To them, this meant dealing with the smaller elements of the design at the outset as part of the hierarchy of the overall scale relationships. The brothers' architectural training at MIT, the strong influence of H. H. Richardson, and the examples from Trinity Church made clear the importance of detail—hardware, texture, furnishings, and color—to an architectural creation. It was not unusual for their earliest tissue sketches of structural details to include a piece of furniture with a vase, complete with flower arrangement. They visualized all aspects of their designs at once, and though these early concepts would be refined, the basic principles remained.

Left: Stairway detail in the main hall.

In the Blacker House, the decorative arts are manifested in the organization of the basic materials and construction details. At every turn, the decorative arts are apparent in the elements of structural joinery, art glass, lighting, woodworking, gold leaf, mural painting, tile inlay, metalwork, and fireplace accessories. The Greenes surrounded themselves with the very finest master craftsmen in each field and held them to the exacting standards they had set for themselves.

Structural Decorative Arts

The Greenes' work clearly resonates the integrity of basic building units, a system for organizing these multiple units, transitions between units, and the forthright expression of the joinery. Nowhere are these four elements more clearly evident than in the Blacker stairway. Each rise of the stair is expressed by the arrangement of the horizontal components of the construction. There is a distinct order and rhythm to their compositions. Each wood member is rolled at the edges to declare its individuality and to express its part in the overall organization of the many parts. The sculptural shaping of timbers introduces points of change, and the square peg acknowledges the blind mortise-and-tenon joinery. Large, rectangular wood pegs control lateral movement; internal wood splines resist the natural tendency of the wood to twist, and finger-lap corner joinery introduces a distinct third dimension to the composition. From the bold scale of the column and timbers, the sculptural shaping of stabilizing corbels, the scale of railing, and the rhythm of its pegging, the Greenes have given to this

design its full range of proportional relationships. Each part is essential to the overall statement. This careful and sensitive composition is an expression of the Greenes' belief in the decorative arts as an integral part of the architecture.

On the exterior, bold wrought-iron straps wrap the built-up timbers of the terrace columns, locking them together with opposing iron wedges. The Greenes' handling of this simple detail adds another dimension to the articulated-timber-construction vocabulary. The Greenes exposed, rather than hid, the methods of their construction, giving to the design a forthright and honest expression.

Wrought-iron strap-and-wedge detail locks the three-post timber terrace column together.

Art Glass

Charles and Henry Greene had incorporated art glass into their work as early as 1897, but it was not until their fortuitous association with glass artisan Emil Lange in 1906 that they were able to fully explore its potential. One principal source of color in the Blacker House is from the art glass of the windows and lighting fixtures.

The art-glass designs for the three north-facing entrance doors are a combination of vertical linear representations of the sun's rays and horizontal clouds. Charles took license to treat these elements as a trellis over which he composed a twisting vine with flowers. The three clerestory windows above the banks of French doors to the rear court on the south have imagery similar to that used in the entry doors, but here without the linear underlay.

For the lanterns, Charles looked to the sky as a source for his lyrical and sometimes geometric compositions of clouds and birds in flight.

The two side doors of the three-part entry doors have screens, allowing breezes to pass through the main hall.

Charles purposely split the grand bay-window art glass at the landing of the stairwell near mid-section. The lower glass panels are deep shades of brown and depict a hexagonal trellis grid with a grapevine intertwined. For privacy, the translucent glass permits little light to enter and illuminate the interior space. The casement windows of the upper section of the bay, which can open to the breezes, have a field of near-transparent golden opalescent glass free of background pattern. This allows the grapevine with its realistic leaf coloration and the intense grape clusters to be featured. The upper set of bay windows is brighter than the lower, and adds considerably more filtered light into the upper hall while also providing privacy.

Leaded-and-stained-glass window in bathroom no. 1.

Greene & Greene drew upon imagery from the gardens for the glass pattern in the bay window of the main stair landing.

For exterior lighting, broad-hooded brass lanterns were designed in several sizes. With time, the brass oxidized to a rich green, contrasting with the brown wood timbers and complementing the green split shakes on the walls.

Left: Bay window at the main stair landing in the hall.

Right: Laminated-glass-and-leading detail in windows in the bay at the main stair landing.

In two of the upstairs bathrooms—no. 2, the master bath, and no. 3, the guest bath—the floral imagery in the art glass is completely representational. Each of these windows adds light as well as maintains privacy between the two interiors, offering the opportunity to experience both transmitted and refracted light. In both cases, the color changes are noticeably exciting.

Right: Bathroom no. 2 interior window as seen from the sunroom.

Far right: Same window lighted from behind.

Right: Glass door panel of bathroom no. 3 from the hall.

Far right: Interior bathroom glass, with leading painted to match the wood trim.

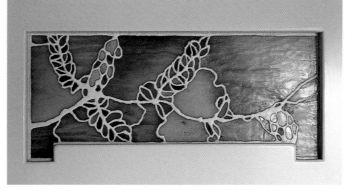

Lighting

Greene & Greene were fascinated with lighting design and approached it in a variety of ways. In the hands of Charles Greene, the new electric lighting was as much the creation of a sculpture in light as it was a source of ambient room light. Task lighting was supplied by floor or table lamps, and the combined effect was muted and consistent with the Greenes' belief that interiors in the hot, arid climate of southern California should present a cool, cave-like quality as a shelter from the heat of the day.

Top left: Main hall lanterns are suspended on leather straps.

The main hall and upper hall lanterns reflect the brothers' interest in Japanese temple imagery. With careful attention given to scale and proportion, there is continuity in the designs of the teak frames and the iridescent art-glass panels. The five lanterns in the entry hall and the one in the upper hall were suspended by leather straps, capturing the viewer's attention.

Right: Six mahogany and leaded-and-stained-glass lanterns, suspended from the ceiling, wash the gesso and gold-leaf relief of the living room with soft light.

Although these lanterns were not designed as task lighting, they did not make a favorable impression on William R. Thorsen's sister, who wrote:

One more point. Don't let Greene light your rooms with lanterns of stained glass. They are very artistic in shape and coloring perceived in the daylight but as points of illumination they are rather negative and one finds oneself in a dim religious light everywhere in the house. . . .

Middle left: The design for the teak wall sconces in the upper hall was repeated in bedrooms no. 3 and no. 4, executed in Port Orford cedar.

In the living room, six lighting baskets of mahogany and art glass suspended from overhead beams wash the ceiling with a soft light. The art-glass panels of these lanterns depict water lilies from the Blackers' lake.

In the guest bedroom, bedroom no. 3, the designs are much simpler than those in the more public rooms, using a stylized cloud configuration at the top and an abstract flower-and-stem detail on the side panels.

In the dining room and the upstairs bedrooms, the Greenes chose wall-mounted lighting sconces that varied slightly from room to room. For the master suite and the dining room sconces, a silk pongee skirt replaced glass as a diffuser of the light.

Bottom left: Wall-sconce lighting in the dining room, with folded skirt of silk pongee.

Broad, shallow light trays are suspended by leather straps from richly detailed mahogany ceiling panels over the dining and breakfast room tables. The mahogany side panels of the light trays are detailed for inserts of thin pieces of iridescent glass to transmit and refract light. The large art-glass bottom panels of the two light trays are geometric design, with floriform panels of glass laminated at the cross points. Attention was given to the color selection of the iridescent glass in order to enhance both the food and the skin tones of those seated at the tables. The original sketches for these light trays show an open bottom with a silk pongee skirt dropping from the edge similar to the wall sconces. This design was changed and the bottom closed to shade the glare of bare lightbulbs.

Woodworking

The characteristics of wood were certainly well known to both Blacker and the Greenes. The effects of water, wind, and sand are a part of the natural aging of wood, providing a texture very different from the effects of cutting wood into boards or hand carving. To accomplish this desired quality, the Greenes selected redwood, a softwood, for the frieze in the upper hall and for the billiard room in the basement. Instead of carving, the Greenes' craftsmen used heavy wire brushes to draw out the soft, summer wood, exposing the three-dimensional pattern of the grain. This weathered, brushed surface was wiped with a light brown stain and treated with a clear, penetrating oil, allowing the natural beauty of the wood to highlight the new texture.

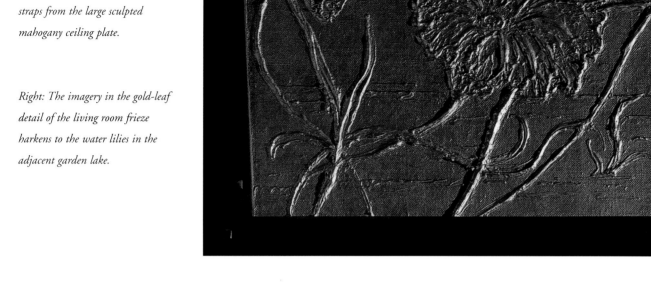

Gesso and Gold Leaf

Greene & Greene were well aware that the California sunshine had a yellow light. When refracting off the glossy surface of the lotus leaf in the Blacker lake, it reflected gold. To bring this experience into the living room, the Greenes experimented with the use of gold-metal leaf in the frieze and corner ceiling detail. The lotus-leaf pattern was carried out in a gesso bas-relief[1] that was covered with golden-colored metal leaf muted by the final surface glazing. Light from the six hanging lanterns washed up onto the golden leaves across the ceiling, revealing the slight imagery of rippling water, also done in gesso and then over-painted with a muted golden brown.

Painted Mural Work

In the restoration of the Blacker House, it became very clear that the dining room is not complete without the addition of the painted murals in the frieze. The range of proportional relationships, scale of detail, color, and texture are essential to the hierarchy of the composition.

1. Gesso: a plaster of paris or gypsum prepared with glue for use in painting or making bas-reliefs.

A soft golden patina was applied to the andirons of bedroom no. 2.

Dining room fireplace with Grueby tile inlay and metal fender designed by Charles Greene.

Left: Living room fireplace.

Fireplace with copper repoussé hood in bedroom no. 4.

Bedroom no. 2 fireplace.

Tile Inlay

Grueby tiles were the principal selection for use on the fireplace surrounds of the living room, dining rooms, and bedrooms no. 2 and no. 4, the master and primary guest bedrooms. Charles was so precise in his selection of the Grueby tile colors, shades, and textures that his drawings for the detail inlay carefully call out each specification by manufacturer's assigned number. The designs for the various fireplaces use the basic grid of the tile as the background geometry, and then the tiles were cut to allow for the differing configurations of inlay.

Fireplace Accessories

The design and making of fireplace accessories for both the Blacker and Thorsen Houses were carried out over several years between January 1911 and November 1914. At least two sets of andirons were created for the Blacker House: a pair in blackened wrought iron for the living room and a more delicate pair for the master bedroom in cast and polished steel with a gold patina.

Unique among the Greene & Greene decorative-arts palette for the Blacker House, brass fenders were executed for each of the four fireplaces. Crafted of sheet brass with a copper-brown patina, the fenders featured different designs with abstract folded-ribbon compositions and others that drew their inspiration from plant materials.

The Blacker living room fireplace was made complete with Charles's elaborate design for its three-part, hinged, folding fire screen. Plant materials from the lake again were chosen as the imagery for the detail of the bronze frame and hinge verticals as well as for the bas-relief of the lower inset panels in brass and copper.

Metalwork

Acting on the suggestion of Nellie Blacker, Charles incorporated the iris and butterflies into the design of the air registers in the three public rooms. Though they varied in size and proportion in the main hall, living room, and dining room, they were fundamentally the same design.

Greene & Greene had developed a distinct style and considered the decorative arts a natural extension and refinement of their architectural designs. In an age of increasing specialization, part of the appeal of their work lies in the versatility of their artistic output, not only evident in the decorative-arts designs for the Blacker House but also particularly exciting in the design and craftsmanship of the largest body of furniture of the Greenes' career.

Metal air registers of the entry hall, living room, and dining room continued the garden imagery.

5

THE FURNITURE

Architects have frequently attempted the design of furniture. Few, however, have been able to transcend the urge to compose their furniture as though each piece were a miniature work of architecture. In the attempt to relate furnishings to the design of the space, it is too often forgotten that architecture and furnishings are two separate entities calling upon differing sensitivities and responses to materials, scale, proportion, and detail. And while architecture and furnishings are but parts of an overall total and unified composition, the integrity of their independent qualities is essential. This Greene & Greene deeply believed.

The Blacker Furniture

A careful study of the Blacker furniture establishes that the Blacker House was created as a personal residence rather than for entertaining. There is no furniture for public use. The furnishings for each room have been specifically designed for the functions in that room and to be placed in a particular location. The most preliminary tissue drawings include notations made during discussions with their clients, the deletions or additions of certain pieces, and precise instructions as to placement. The purpose and degree of specific detail for each furniture design is evocative of the close working relationship between Charles Greene and Nellie Blacker. The Greenes were so convincing in their proposal to the Blackers that they were able to design the complete complement of furniture for the principal rooms of the Blacker House—main hall, living room, and dining/breakfast room—and a few pieces for the master bedroom.

Charles's early tissue sketches for the Blacker furniture, with his personal pencil notations, were sent over to the Hall shops for comment on 1 July 1908 and stamped "Return to Greene & Greene, Architects, 215 Boston Bldg., Pasadena, Cal." The returned sketches with additional notes by John Hall affix a number to each furniture design and the quantity to be made.

Main hall exhibiting original Greene & Greene furniture.

The Main Hall

While the main hall was the entry to the house, the place where friends would have been greeted, it was more a room where the Blackers spent a considerable amount of their time. From here, by virtue of the selection of furniture and its specific placement facing the rear courtyard, the Blackers could enjoy the fountain and head-pond of the lake, as well as the vista of the south gardens featuring the seasonal change of color from the flowers in Mrs. Blacker's prized cutting garden.

The subtle Oriental theme of the main hall is expressed sparingly in the end shaping of the heavy beams, the carved volute detail of the furniture legs, the corbel of the stairway column, and in the "lift" of the lighting lantern hoods. These furnishings are carried out in teak.

Unique to the Blacker House are the two case pieces for the main hall, each featuring outdoor scenes of mountains, trees, lake, and clouds in the hand-carved-teak door panels. The taller of the two case pieces was identified as "Case for S. E. Corner of Hall" and features a single central cupboard with richly carved door and four drawers on each side. The carving in this case is a literal representation of the imagery in Charles's conceptual tissue sketch. The smaller of the cases is identified on the tissue drawings as "table with cupboards and drawers—to be set against the west wall of hall near entrance." It has two side cupboards with carved doors and two central drawers. The carved doors are more abstract in their representation of clouds and lakeshore. Shorter than the other case, it has an unattached vertical mirror hung by leather straps from the hanging rail above. The two pieces form a balanced composition.

The differences between the two cases in the refinement of the design and the hand carvings of the doors are dramatic and indicate that two different craftsmen worked on the cases. The literal execution of the door in the larger case suggests its being made earlier than the smaller one, allowing Charles time to rethink the detail and composition of its two doors.

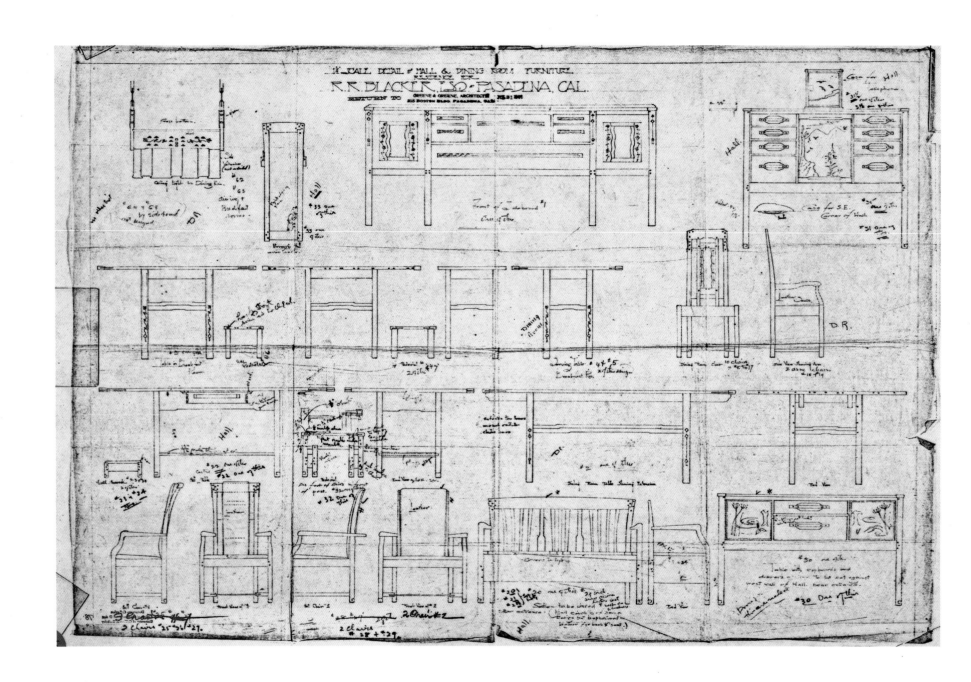

Initial drawings for the larger case illustrate a small cabinet on the top. The birds-in-flight imagery for its door carving was used in the leaded-glass panels of the five hanging lanterns in the hall.

Two designs were made for the main hall chairs: a high-back armchair and a very broad-fronted, more casual chair. Both designs are upholstered in golden brown leather. Three of the first designs were made to be used around the perimeter of the hall.

These have a slightly flared back with typical Greene & Greene ebony spline and square pegs joining the leg to the top rail. The narrow leather splat accentuates the high back, giving to the chair an elegant simplicity.

The second chair design for the main hall has similar detailing in the arms and legs but has an exaggerated broad front width and a standard rear width, causing the sides of the chair to be splayed.

Original Greene & Greene tissue drawing of proposed furniture for the main hall and dining room.

On the original tissue, the back is fixed. In actual fabrication, Charles had redesigned the chair to have an adjustable back in the same fashion as the proverbial "Morris chair." In a typical move on Charles's part, he seems to have taken great joy in celebrating the adjustable-back mechanism. He drew attention to the square, raised, brass lag screws for the various positions of the adjustable back, and reinforced the theme established by the geometric organization of the chair's ebony square-peg joinery.

Designed to be used casually in the center of the main hall adjacent to the large hall table, the Morris-type chair was adapted for the execution of a long matching couch at the request of the Blackers. They had, by then, decided that they would use the main hall for casual sitting.

A small settle with storage space under the hinged seat was designed as a shoe bench for the west wall of the main hall, to the right of the entry doors. The solid teakwood seats could be lifted, providing storage space for boots or other seasonal footwear. Its design follows the principles of the hall furniture, except that the broad back is made up of a series of curving splats. Its storage space requirement necessitated a broad front stretcher and likely influenced this feature in the design of the long, adjustable-back Morris couch.

Three small pieces fill out the main hall furniture. A small pedestal table with inset marble top was created for the placement of a potted plant against the rich warm tones of the teakwood paneling. Two leather-cushioned hassocks were made to keep drafts off the feet when seated at the central table.

Left: High-back main hall chair.

Right: Three Greene & Greene Blacker House chairs: left to right, main hall, bedroom no. 2, living room.

Left: Armed rocking chairs and table in bedroom no. 1.

Right: Back-splat detail and tree-of-life inlay in chair for bedroom no. 2.

The Living Room

The living room furnishings are executed in mahogany with a dark rubbed-oil finish. Unlike the hall pieces, they have an abstract pine-needle inlay of fruitwood, copper, and silver. This suite of furniture initially consisted of a table, a "portable (table) lamp," as it was called out on the drawings, a small couch, four different types of chairs, a writing desk, a music case, a bookcase, and a hassock. At a later date, the Blackers found need for a much larger version of the living room couch, and this was placed in front of the north window.

The living room table is essentially a library table. This magnificent piece of furniture is the anchor of the room arrangement, separating the intimate seating group around the fireplace from the wall of French doors leading to the east terrace. Fitted with three drawers on one side, its low stretchers that stabilize the eight legs restrict its being used as a writing desk.

Archival photograph of living room, ca. 1910.

Archival photograph of dining room, ca. 1910.

Dining room serving table.

Bedroom No. 2

For the master bedroom suite, Charles Greene created two of his most extraordinary and elegant furniture compositions. These similar designs evolved from the need for dressing-room storage, and both pieces were identified on the drawings as "dresser and chiffonier." The side elevations of the two pieces are the same. One has the capacity for the hanging of long garments in the center and for medium and small drawer storage on the sides. The companion piece provides for more drawer space, a narrow dresser top, and a central cupboard for shelving. In their massing and form, these two designs hearken to the furniture designs of the Greenes' Scottish contemporary, Charles Rennie Mackintosh.

Other bedroom pieces include two rocking chairs; a large writing table; a most unusual couch with solid, vertical, upholstered back, sides, and seat; and a small table with a drawer. The tree-of-life theme is carried out abstractly in fruitwood, silver, and copper in all the bedroom furniture.

Robert and Nellie Blacker had given Charles Greene the latitude to expand his furniture vocabulary to another level, as had Adelaide Tichenor in 1904. There were over sixty pieces of furniture and fifty-three lighting fixtures for the Blacker House when Charles Robert Ashbee visited with Charles Greene in 1909. Many of these would have been in various stages of completion in the Halls' shops, along with pieces for other clients. As one of the leading designers, craftsmen, and observers of the Arts & Crafts movement here and in his native England, Ashbee's account[1] of his American tour may tell more about the Greenes, and particularly about the Blacker furnishings, than any other source. He wrote:

Left: Chiffonier for bedroom no. 2, featuring the "tree of life" inlay.

Right: Side chair for bedroom no. 2.

I think C. Sumner Greene's work beautiful, among the best there is in this country. Like Frank Lloyd Wright the spell of Japan is on him, he feels the beauty and makes magic of the horizontal line, but there is in his work more tenderness, more subtlety, more self effacement than in Wright's work. It is more refined and has more repose. Perhaps it loses in strength, perhaps it is California that speaks rather than Illinois, anyway as work is, so far as the interiors go, more sympathetic to me. . . .

. . . He [C. Sumner Greene] took us to . . . [the Hall] workshops where they were making without exception, the best and most characteristic furniture I have seen in this country. There were beautiful cabinets and chairs of walnut and lignum vitae, exquisite doweling and pegging, and in all a supreme feeling for the material, quite up to the best in our English craftsmanship, Spooner, the Barnslys, Lutyens, Lethaby. I have not felt so at home in any workshop on this side of the Atlantic. . . . Here things were really alive and the Arts & Crafts that the others were screaming and hustling about, are here actually being produced by a young architect, this quiet, dreamy, nervous, tenacious little man, fighting single-handedly until recently against tremendous odds.

1. Personal notes courtesy Robert W. Winter, 1968. A more complete excerpt from Ashbee's quotation is published in Robert Winter, "American Sheaves from C. R. A.," *Journal of the Society of Architectural Historians,* December 1971.

6

The perception of architecture as a living art is constantly adjusting to light, unfolding to movement, differing by individual interpretation, and altering by time as a fourth dimension. Herein, Brad Pitt brings these dynamics to his vision of the moods of the Blacker House through his lens and his studied print compositions.

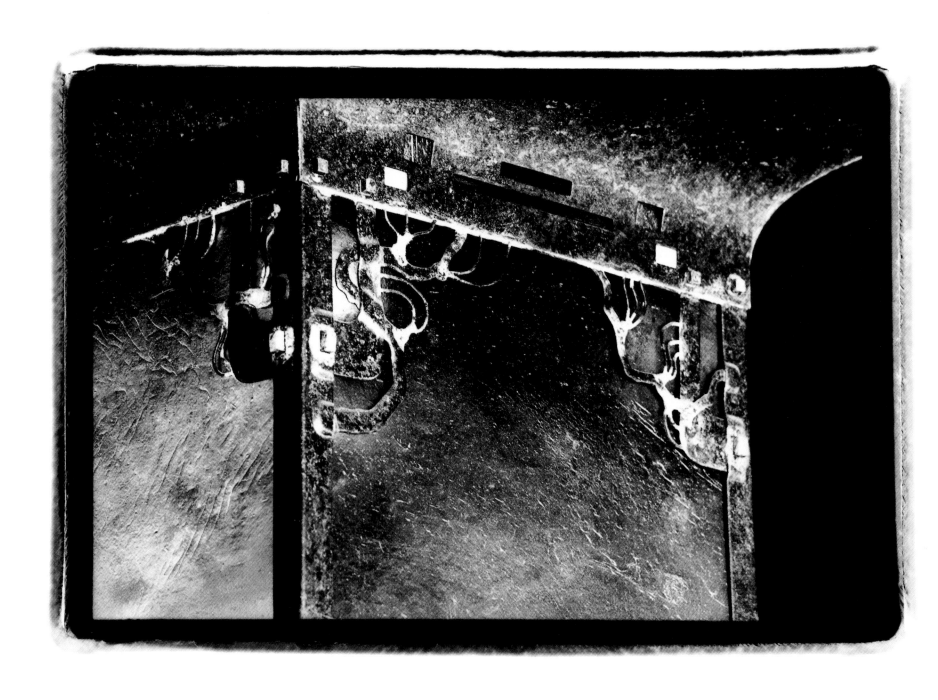

Henry Greene could not have been more prophetic about the future of the Blacker House when he wrote to Charles at his home and studio in Carmel, California, in February of 1942:

I called on Mrs. Blacker and found her feeble but able to be about. . . . I asked her what she would do with the furniture when she passed on. She replied she did not know. I suggested she place some of the finer pieces in some good museum where students and art lovers could see it. She made no answer to this.

Mrs. Blacker's love of her home was well known. She had worked closely with Charles Greene on the details and furnishings of the house, and, following Robert Blacker's death on 16 September 1931, had engaged Henry Greene to check the house and grounds periodically and arrange for the appropriate maintenance. In Nellie's hands the Blacker estate adhered to the high standards initially set by Huntington and his associates when they developed Oak Knoll. In another part of the letter to Charles, Henry wrote:

Mrs. Blacker said she had great joy living there. . . . She has a companion with her all the time. She asked to be remembered to you. The place looks lovely now with the green lawns and trees and shrubbery, vistas, bird bath and pool. The inside of the house is perfect yet; apparently not a scar or shrinkage or blemish. Quite a number of years ago I had Savage go over all the woodwork and furniture; and so it looks and is as smooth as velvet yet. . . .

On 22 May 1946, Nellie Canfield Blacker passed away. She left the house and the carefully manicured 5.1 acres of grounds in perfect condition, complete with all of its furnishings and lighting fixtures. The thought that it would ever be changed was inconceivable. She had given considerable thought to Henry Greene's concern about the furniture and had stipulated that the contents be sold with the house. Unfortunately, those provisions were ill conceived, for the stipulations did not carry over to subsequent ownerships, and a devastating series of events took place.

As control of the property passed from the hands of the Blacker family, successive owners began to impose on the once-proud flagship of Oak Knoll one change after another that deprived the exteriors, interiors, and grounds of the dignity and unity the Blackers and Greenes had envisioned.

Reproductions of two of fifty-three Greene & Greene lighting fixtures, designed and made specifically for the Blacker House, that were removed from the house on 3 May 1985.

Overleaf: West elevation.

The Estate Divided

In little more than a year after Nellie Blacker's death, five parties banded together, purchased the estate, and began the process of subdividing the property. On 14 November 1947, documents for the subdivision were filed, creating seven separate parcels. The official subdivision recording of tract 15093 occurred less than three months later on 28 January 1948.

The Blacker main house was separated from its outhouses (secondary structures) on the new parcel no. 1. The garage occupied parcel no. 2; and the keeper's house and lathhouse, parcel no. 3. Parcels no. 4 through no. 7 were created by the removal of the lake, its tributary basins, the pergola, and the balance of the gardens. Some time later, parcel No. 7 was split and another house built five feet from the new east property line of the Blacker House.

The impact of this subdivision on the Blacker House was devastating. The new eastern side-yard property line was cut so close to the massive three-level structure that the house was strangled on its tight site. So eager were the investors to squeeze more building sites out of the Blacker estate that they gave little consideration to the main house and its secondary buildings. To the rear of the Blacker House, the new property line cut through the elegant timbered garden pergola between the house and the garage, thus destroying the vista from the main hall of the house down through the cutting gardens. Little of the rear yard and only two-thirds of the pergola remained.

There was now no garage for the Blacker House. Incredibly, for such a distinguished location, the prevailing city ordinances allowed the porte cochere to satisfy parking requirements, a disastrous decision that let the front yard be used as a parking lot (a factor long considered to be a sign of downgrading in any neighborhood). The highly articulated timber porte cochere was relegated to a tract-house carport. No longer able to serve its proper purpose as an elegant point of arrival and departure, even the presence of a Rolls Royce or a Mercedes Benz was tacky under the grand porte cochere.

The garage with its chauffeur's quarters received a new wing and was converted into a separate residence. Good fortune has retained many of the original spaces, including the garage space itself and its classic broad, swinging Greene & Greene doors.

On parcel no. 3 the Greene & Greene lathhouse succumbed to the blade of a bulldozer to provide yard space for the keeper's house, now converted into a separate residence and property. The Blacker garage and the keeper's house were the first properties to be converted to single-family residences. Over the years, both the garage and the keeper's house have undergone additions and alterations by various owners attempting to honor the integrity of the original Greene & Greene designs. Vacant parcels no. 4 and 5 saw new construction in 1949, and parcels no. 6 and 7 in 1951 and 1953.

But the loss of the gardens to create four new parcels for speculative gain was devastating not only to the Blacker House but also to the center of the entire Oak Knoll neighborhood. The last vestige of the Oak Knoll Ranch qualities that had given the area a uniqueness that contributed substantially to the maintenance of property values was stripped away. Save for the serpentine configuration of street patterns of the original 1886 design that followed the undulating terrain where sheep once grazed and that was interpreted in principle by the Greenes, Oak Knoll would never be the same again.

The Blacker House

While the Blacker main house was spared demolition or alteration following the initial subdivision of the property, it soon began to undergo changes that dramatically affected the integrity of its historic architectural design. In accord with Nellie Blacker's wishes, the Blacker House was sold complete with its furniture, lighting, carpets, silver, and other furnishings. She believed that she had addressed the concerns that Henry Greene had posed some years earlier. However, those stipulations were not legally binding beyond the sale of the property to the first group.

As a result, the first buyer of the Blacker House on parcel no. 1 was free to sell off any and all of the contents of the house. And, much to the consternation of his family, that is exactly what he did: he conducted a yard sale. The furniture was the first to go.

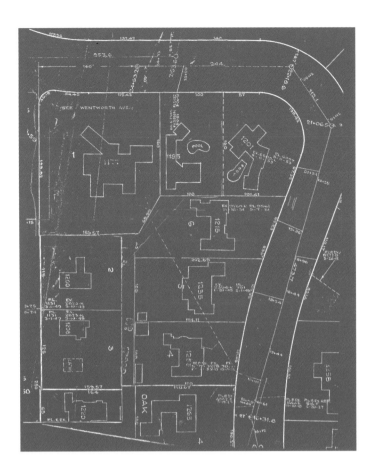

Subdivision map of the Blacker estate.

There was no attempt to promote this furniture as specially designed for the Blacker House, and there was no special market at the time for Greene & Greene–designed furniture. It was purely a salable commodity. During the yard sale, a large portion of the furniture was purchased by one buyer, and for many years these pieces were housed in the neighborhood just a few doors away from the Blacker House. As renewed respect for the works of Greene & Greene developed, this collection came to be looked on as an investment and was carefully merchandised, a few pieces at a time. Today the Blacker furniture is distributed throughout the country and overseas in museums, private collections, and antiques stores.

Over the years, well-intentioned owners attempted to maintain the Blacker House, but ill-advised techniques and materials only exacerbated the problems. The house continued to deteriorate: rafter tails rotted, pieces hung off the ends or fell off, dry rot set in, and the posts and outriggers checked and cracked. Roofs were applied incorrectly over too many totally disintegrated previous roofs that were incapable of supporting the new one. In an attempt to cover the discoloration resulting from prior conditions of the exterior, each new painter applied any number of unknown materials over the problem areas. The lyrical color scheme that acknowledged the role of the various materials and elements of the original construction was gone. The soft brown stain expressing the natural grain of the timber was covered over and over again with unknown black substances. The new and untreated replacement redwood shakes of decades prior had turned black. The natural blond frames of the window screens had also turned black.

The entire character, scale, and dignity were ultimately stripped from the Blacker House. The once-light, airy, and colorful architectural landmark with its free-flowing grounds was now a dark, heavy, lumbering eyesore on its limited corner site with its graceful entry drive used as a parking lot.

On 1 May 1985, escrow closed on the purchase of the Blacker House by buyers who had convinced the seller of their intention to restore and occupy the house. Within hours, all window coverings in the house were drawn and over fifty lighting fixtures removed from ceilings and walls. In the dark of night, separate shipping crates carefully crafted to fit each of the lighting fixtures were delivered, and in three-days' time large moving vans were loaded and on their way to Texas. The Blacker House had been raped of its fifty-three Greene & Greene lighting fixtures.

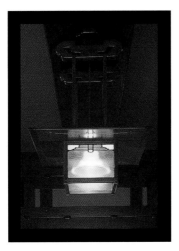

Impetus for Preservation Acts

Across the nation, historians and preservationists were outraged. Within days, the City of Pasadena passed a temporary city ordinance drafted to protect Greene & Greene structures from being pillaged and parted out. This was a wake-up call addressing every historic structure of merit. Headlines across the country decried the act, but few had answers suggesting the necessary means to protect a property against similar acts in the future. City officials, representatives of preservation organizations, and individuals went to Texas and New York in an attempt to reason and negotiate with the buyer. The National Trust for Historic Preservation focused on the issue at its national meeting in Seattle in October of 1985, and made a $20,000 commitment to Pasadena Heritage, whose organization was attempting to find persons who would purchase the Blacker House. Following the Seattle conference, the owner refused all further attempts to negotiate with the City of Pasadena or its preservation organizations.

Meanwhile, Pasadena residents became involved in a heated controversy over the wording of a permanent preservation ordinance (dubbed the Blacker Ordinance) aimed at providing some form of protection from the parting-out of historic structures. In the end, a watered-down version was put in place, calling for a counter review of alterations of all buildings over fifty years old and, in the case of landmark structures, a delay in the removal of parts or demolition for specified periods. This would allow for attempts at preservation resolutions beneficial to the owner as well as in the best interests of stabilizing neighborhood property values that are distinctly impacted by architectural treasures.

When finally enacted in mid-1987, the Blacker Ordinance affected the Blacker House as well. The same owners who removed the lighting fixtures requested approval to remove the art-glass windows and doors. The request was denied by the city's new Cultural Heritage Commission, prompting a continuing watch of all activity at the Blacker House. Eventually, an agreement was negotiated that allowed the owner to remove the original art-glass windows and doors and replace them with exact reproductions on condition that he not remove any other parts from the house. While this resolution was not satisfactory to the architectural community, it did prevent the removal of additional interior elements and the sale of complete rooms.

On 23 June 1988 the owner entered into an agreement with private individuals in Pasadena for the sale of the Blacker House with the reproduction doors and windows but without any lighting fixtures. For the moment, the tired nation was somewhat set at ease. It appeared the Blacker House was in good hands with owners who were familiar with the neighborhood, who wished to restore the house and make it a home for their young family. However, six years later the Blacker House was again up for sale.

The ability for young minds to study the genius of this residence was denied. The pride that this art form gave the community and the inspiration to the artistic endeavors of the culture were nearly gone. The prospects for the future maintenance of the Blacker House seemed possible, though it looked unlikely that new owners with an inspired vision of the significance of the original artistic merit would come forward. The Blacker House, as a beacon of artistic achievement, it seemed, would never exist again. At a terrible cost, a nation had been awakened.

THE RESTORATION

Ellen and Harvey Knell missed the opportunity to purchase the Blacker House in May of 1985. They had always admired it for its masterful timber construction and articulated joinery. Their long association with the building-materials business and their love of wood and an appreciation for the craftsmanship in the construction of sailing vessels naturally drew them to the architecture of Greene & Greene. When the Henry M. Robinson estate[1] came on the market in November of 1993, the Knells quickly entered into escrow for the purchase of the historic property. In a letter enumerating their serious plans for the restoration of the house, they stated: ". . . one objective in this project would be to do a first-class job of restoring the house. . . . We really want to do the job right. We very much like the Craftsman style and would like the feeling of being part of preserving a significant Greene & Greene work. . . ."

During the escrow, research began on the Robinson project; planning for the restoration was carried out and drawings were prepared for submission to the Pasadena City Cultural Heritage Commission. Eight months later on 6 June 1994, the proposals for the restoration were lauded by the commission and given enthusiastic approval, but the Robinson purchase dropped out of escrow. The Knells' dreams were celebrated and destroyed on the same day.

Peeling finishes, resulting from years of improper maintenance, and rotting conditions of the once richly timbered pergola are dramatic reminders of the decrepit condition of the Blacker House prior to the Knells' meticulous restoration, begun in 1994.

Fortuitously, within weeks the Blacker House was placed on the market. The Knells were quick to enter into a short escrow for its purchase and eager to use the experience of the Robinson House on the research and planning for the project that would change their lives.

The restoration of the Blacker House is a story of enlightened vision, passion, and teamwork. As it was for the original design and construction of the estate, there was need for a close involvement of owners, restoration architect, and master craftsmen, all committed to the high standards set by Greene & Greene, in the restoration of this landmark building and in carrying out such improvements as to justify the effort and the expenditure of funds in providing for the needs of a new generation. At the outset, it was clear that no complete plan for the full restoration work would be possible until certain portions

1. The Henry M. Robinson House, built in 1905, was the Greenes' second-largest estate property in Pasadena.

of the house were opened up and investigated. At the same time, it was essential that sufficient drawings and specifications be developed to ascertain a general working budget and warrant the issuance of a building permit. Meetings were held with officials of the Pasadena Department of Building and Safety to bring their expertise to the team. It was the working together of all parties that made possible the quality of the completed restoration.

The Blacker restoration was to be an endeavor that was a joy to everyone concerned. The owners therefore established certain understandings: the restoration had to be economically sound; time was to be spent on the investigation and development of new techniques better suited for particular tasks; any savings achieved by these new techniques were to be used to advance other parts of the restoration; the owners would function as their own general contractor, being involved in all of the decisions and being represented on a daily basis by their appointed project manager working closely with the restoration architect and key craftsmen.

Initial planning for the restoration of the Blacker House and grounds addressed earthquake concerns, rotted wood structural members, returning the exterior surfaces to their original color and finish, fencing the property, and carefully studying the now-limited grounds. On the interiors, the program included restoring and slightly modifying the kitchen and bathrooms; removing hazardous materials; upgrading electrical, plumbing, and heating systems; adding air-conditioning; cleaning and refinishing wood surfaces; reestablishing gold-leaf detail in the living room; and re-creating original lighting fixtures and some Greene & Greene furniture previously removed from the house.

There were no plans for removing the roof or the redwood shakes on the exterior walls, or for completely stripping the exterior to bare wood. However, within a few weeks it became clear that all this needed to be done. Each phase in its own way was necessary to carry out the work of the others. The rafter restoration affected the roof, the paints on the wood affected the rafter work, the shakes on the walls affected the paint removal, and the removal of wall shakes opened new access for the electrical, plumbing, and other services. No part of the house went untouched.

The restoration in process, 1994.

Rotting Rafter Tails and Outriggers

In order to restore and properly finish more than three hundred rafter tails and outrigger beams that had rotted, checked, or fallen off, it was necessary to splice on solid wood milled from dismantled bridge timbers. These were old-growth Oregon pine, naturally dry from age, and were compatible with the sound wood of the existing structure. While other methods of reconstituting the ends of the rotted timbers would not produce the desired finish, adding new wood created new projections of rafters and outriggers that would be able to respond uniformly to the transparent penetrating-oil stains.

The newly milled rafter and beam ends were cut in a single diagonal scarf joint to afford a more uniform fit to the reverse cut of the old timbers and assure a tight bond of the epoxy adhesive. To strengthen the larger outriggers, steel rods placed on a reverse diagonal were inserted into the two parts encased in epoxy. To protect against future rot, the splice needed to be under the eaves, protected from the elements; thus, it was necessary to pull the roof back to the line of the exterior wall. That investigation determined that the last roof had been applied to plywood nailed to earlier roofs that were now rotted to dust; the existing roof was not actually fastened to the structure of the house.

Exterior Finishes

The testing of several paint and stain products on the wood surfaces yielded unsatisfactory results. The placement of yet another product on top of existing coatings produced a finished surface not worthy of the investment in the entire project. It was therefore necessary to strip the exterior structure to bare wood and work back to achieve the original Greene & Greene color, texture, and protective finish.

With the exterior structural members clean, the next task was to re-create the Cabot transparent penetrating-oil stain. By lifting off a piece of trim or examining particles of original stains, identifying the colors was relatively easy. With testing done in Pasadena and in consultation with chemists at the Cabot factories in the East, it was possible to match the original color and quality using environmentally friendly products made by Cabot today.

Re-milled old bridge timbers were used for the restoration of the rotted rafter tails.

Tests of semitransparent stain on unstripped wood demonstrated that such results were unsatisfactory and would not justify the monetary investment for the restoration.

Matching the original colors and textures became one of the most significant visual aspects of the entire restoration project. To Greene & Greene, the expression of the role of the various exterior materials was important to their architectural style. Research revealed that structural timbers and beams were stained a medium brown and wall shakes a strong green. Redwood roof shakes were left natural; window, screen, and door frames were left blond with natural oil finishes; and the innate colors of rolled roofing, aged copper, and wrought iron were allowed to take on their natural colors and patinas. In the hands of Greene & Greene, the combination of these colors and stains formed an exterior palette for the Blacker House that was in sharp contrast to the somber black of the exterior prior to restoration.

The reinstatement of the color and exterior finishes of the Blacker House has provided the first opportunity in over half a century to experience the true exterior of a Greene & Greene house as it was originally built.

Exterior Wall Shakes

The redwood shakes that had been specially split and installed on the house less than two decades earlier had turned black and were dry and cracking as a result of being unprotected. The decision to remove the shakes was also beneficial because opening the exterior walls provided direct access for electrical, plumbing, and air-duct work, not only relieving the great costs of altering the interiors for such work but also avoiding the removal and alteration of meticulous interior woodwork.

With the removal of rotted roofs and the shakes off the exterior walls, more effective methods became available for removing paint and other unknown materials from the entire structure. Following the testing of numerous products and working with manufacturers in the United States and Canada, a spray process was selected to remove surface materials in an expeditious and economical way.

Above: Color as a factor in the differentiation of elements of the structure was essential to the Greene & Greene Style.

Installation of shakes treated with the transparent penetrating-oil stain on raw wood.

Earthquake Work

While the Blacker House had survived a lifetime of earthquakes with little effect, the owners chose to respond to the considerable new knowledge recent California quakes have revealed relating to the differences between lateral and vertical movement. Older structures close to epicenters of the quake have been moved off their foundations when there has not been a strong tie between the frame of the house and the foundation. While current building codes do not require additional structural work for earthquakes, the amount of investment in the complete restoration necessitated such work be done.

Removing the shakes off the walls opened up the structure for more efficient solutions to the various earthquake concerns. The engineer could much better assess options and design for the several different conditions. At points where the heavy wood sill was exposed on the exterior, steel anchors were inserted, binding the house to the masonry foundation. Where terraces flanked the house, the earthquake work—locking the structure of the house onto the wood joist system and anchoring it to the brick foundation wall—had to be accomplished entirely from the interior basement. In most instances, these basement earthquake ties were incorporated into the detailing of the new media room developed from the original basement and furnace area. At openings for under-floor air vents, steel channels were used to tie the house to the foundation in order to maintain the integrity of the Greene & Greene brick detail.

Fencing

Fencing the property was a major challenge. The visual impact of the fence materials and configuration would bring significant change to the Greene & Greene design. The solution was to make the fence disappear. In response to the Greenes' original landscape terracing as well as safety and security concerns, the fence configuration was stepped and kept tight to the house. Most important, the fence design was kept as open as possible so that the vista of the house would appear unchanged.

The Blacker House was originally designed as a highly articulated timber kiosk resting freely in the midst of a natural park. It had no constraints. With the considerable amount of property having been sold off, such enclosure posed a real intrusion on the design of the house. Working directly with wrought-iron fabricators from the beginning, a design drawn from the essence of other Greene & Greene ironwork in Pasadena was developed and detailed in such a way that, through the use of repetitive elements and simplified construction detail, the costs were made affordable. The manner of fastening the wrought iron was limited to solid iron straps heated on installation, allowing for natural rust protection and the uniformity that will come from aging. Thus, there are no weld spots, no requirement for periodic maintenance, and the ironwork will weather in the same manner as that built by Greene & Greene.

The Grounds

As the project proceeded, sentiments changed regarding the landscaping of the grounds. It was agreed that any form of new landscape plan would be seen as foreign. Instead, careful observation was made of archival photographs. As a result, the restoration work on the grounds consisted primarily of removing a significant amount of landscaping planted by later owners. This allowed the small area of grounds remaining around the Blacker House to be as open as possible. The important original roll and terracing of the lawns established by the Greenes has been subtly maintained in the front yard.

Lengthy discussions resulted in the conclusion that almost any added landscape material would draw attention away from the beauty of the structure and emphasize the space problems created by the subdivision of the estate.

Above: The required new wrought-iron fence was designed to disappear, allowing the full view of the elevation of the house to be retained.

Above right: The miracle finishes popular in the 1950s had to be removed to gain access to the wood to restore the original finishes and color.

Below right: Main hall wood panels after restoration.

The Interiors

There was a strong desire to reverse any changes made to the design, to finish surfaces and to detailing of the interiors of the Blacker House that had taken place after Mrs. Blacker's death. They occurred primarily in the kitchen, screened porch, master bathroom, and living room frieze. Painted surfaces throughout the house had undergone much change over the years and some of the original canvas had unfortunately been removed. Popularly merchandised finishes, sold to consumers as miracle polishes to brighten up wood surfaces, had been used in the living and dining rooms. Since these artificial finishes had to be completely removed, the need for restoration in some of these areas offered the opportunity to insert contemporary amenities within the vocabulary of the Greene & Greene Style.

Another challenge resulted from the owners' requirement that their dogs have access to the house through the service areas. City codes would not permit a fence beyond the west face of the house where the logical access door to the original service porch, adjacent to the kitchen, was located. However, pressed by the setback-code restriction, an alternative route was found. By inserting a door into the original servants' dining room, relocating its connecting door to the porch, and converting the space to a service porch primarily for matters related to the two large dogs, access to the rear yard was possible along a new path below the dining room windows and was connected by the addition of a new bridge across the existing basement stairwell. Since the new path along the side of the house is recessed, the new wrought-iron fence does not rise above the bottom of the dining room windows and so maintains the vista of the west garden from the interior.

The original screened porch between the servants' dining room and the kitchen had been enclosed with fixed clear-glass windows at some time, and the detailing was not consistent with the house. These windows were redesigned to relate to the house; the door and window to the kitchen were removed and the original screened porch was converted to a breakfast porch open to the kitchen.

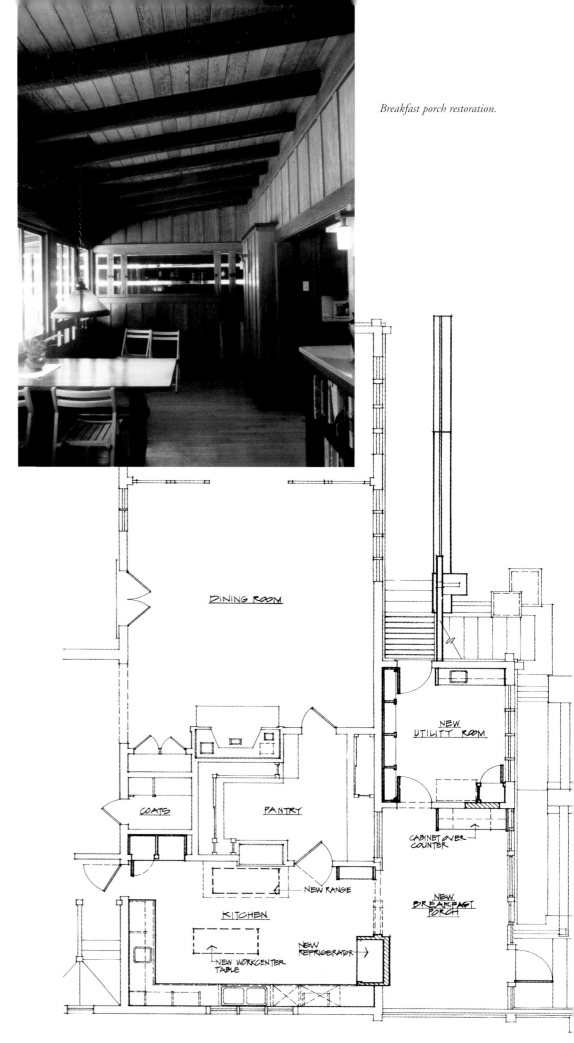

Breakfast porch restoration.

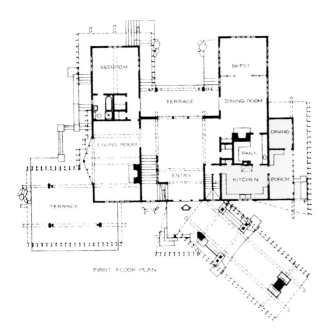

Original plan of first floor.

Restoration plan of kitchen and screened porch.

116

The kitchen had been altered on several occasions over the years. The owners desired to restore the kitchen and, at the same time, design within the Greene & Greene aesthetic some conveniences needed for modern living. Counters were replaced with naturally finished pine. A small closet received a double oven, and space was acquired for the refrigerator by creating a recess in the wall between the breakfast porch and the kitchen. Wood detail and trim in the kitchen were restored to their original natural finish, and paint colors were researched and matched to those originally applied. By inserting thin task-lighting fixtures under the wall cabinets and others over the top for ambient lighting, the original four drop lights fitted with holophane clear-glass shades proved more than adequate for contemporary demands.

In the master bathroom suite, bathroom no. 2 had suffered considerable change in character due to the removal of the footed bathtub and replacement with a Jacuzzi tub, the addition of an adjacent stall shower, and the removal of the original sitz bath. The strong desire to restore the bath to its original state and to add a second pedestal sink, walk-in shower, and Jacuzzi room posed another design challenge. By making the rear portion of the adjacent walk-in closet part of the bathroom, both goals were met. Due to prior changes, it was necessary to have the three-by-six-inch white tiles on the walls custom produced. This allowed also for the new shower room to match the original bathroom. A matching pedestal sink and faucets were located and inserted into the original bathroom design. An additional medicine cabinet and wall-sconce light fixture were crafted to match the existing. The two-by-two-inch-hexagonal white floor tiles were available, and these were used in both the new shower room and the restoration of the bath.

The plumbing system was completely updated in copper pipe. Every effort was made to use the original faucets. Throughout the house, the bathtubs and sinks were rusted at their drains. Rather than applying artificial patch repairs, a nationwide search produced a manufacturer in the Los Angeles area who would remove the existing finish and re-porcelain the entire units. The process was indeed fascinating. However, the high temperatures in the ovens warped and distorted the tubs and sink tops and several were rendered unusable. It became necessary, therefore, to seek out matching sinks and tubs from used-parts suppliers. All of the

hardware and fittings for tubs and sinks in the house were dismantled, replated with the original nickel silver finish, refitted with working parts, and reinstalled. In almost all cases, the original hardware was refurbished and reused. In a few instances, new products were available that were very close to the originals specified by the Greenes.

In the master suite, a dressing room existed between the master bedroom and bathroom no. 2. With the removal of the rear portion of the walk-in closet for the shower room, the remaining portion became a wardrobe opening directly off the dressing room. For additional hanging space, a dual-facing low wardrobe cabinet was designed for the center of the room. Access could be made from each side, creating individual dressing spaces. On each opposite wall of the dressing room, built-in cabinets containing drawers were carried out to match the Greene & Greene detailing in the Blacker House. This arrangement of the central low wardrobes and the banks of storage drawers created individual dressing spaces. By keeping the height of the central dual wardrobe cabinet to forty-eight inches, the spaciousness and natural-light qualities of the original space were maintained.

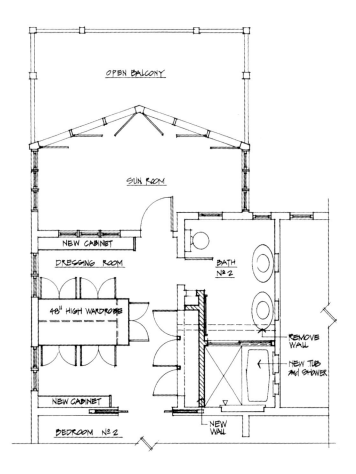

Original plan of second floor.

Restoration plan of bathroom no. 2 and dressing room.

Throughout the process of opening up parts of the house to gain access for work on the electrical, plumbing, and heating, care was taken to identify hazardous materials. Specialized contractors were brought in and all such substances removed. Even beyond the rules of building codes, this was a house with many years of living in its future, and concerns for the health of upcoming generations were foremost on the minds of all involved with the restoration and its processes. To upgrade the electrical supply and distribution, a large new panel measuring seven feet wide, six feet six inches high, and sixteen inches deep was installed. Large transformers were partially buried. Normal building-code practices would have required that the new equipment be placed openly in the gardens. Working carefully with representatives of the city, ways were found to meet the needs of the Water and Power Department and also honor the integrity of the Greene & Greene house design. Much of the wiring within the walls was still in good order and therefore left in place. In upgrading the electrical systems for safety and security, and to meet the needs of a new era, steps were taken to maintain the visual integrity of the original electrical fittings.

As a part of the extensive restoration of the all-wooden structure, serious attention was devoted to the control and handling of air, temperature, and humidity. While the original gravity-flow furnace system was zoned by virtue of the several separately operating heating units, these would not function compatibly with any new air-cooling system. Mechanical engineers and the restoration team explored varied approaches to a new system that would negate the need for as many as seven independent air condensers positioned in the west garden.

Bathroom no. 2, adjusted and restored.

The system designed was composed of ten independent fan coils secreted in the basement and the attic and tied into a single chiller in the basement; one end of the attic was sectioned off into a separate room acting as a plenum and exhaust for warm air. The final design not only addressed the needs of the house but also made use of the existing duct system for return air while requiring the installation of new ducts for supply. The return-air ducts maintained use of the registers original to the house, while the new air-supply registers were placed in the floor or ceiling. In certain portions of the main floor, the new registers were designed and crafted in oak matching the floors.

The opening of walls during the restoration was kept to a minimum.

Wood surfaces of beams, timbers, and paneling throughout the house, which had been dull and lifeless for some time, received a thorough cleaning that brought forth surprising subtleties in the original tones and colors of the woods. For example, the ceiling of the main hall, carried out completely in wood, has a distinct hierarchy to the changes of color and value between the heavy timber structural beams, the frames of the panel units, the paneling itself, and the square-peg detail of its joinery. The final application of a hand-rubbed oil finish gave to the interiors the soft, natural luster of well-nourished, hand-polished wood.

Detail of ceiling panels in main hall.

Restored dining room.

Dining room looking into the breakfast room.

In the first investigations for the restoration of the living room frieze, conservators discovered that it was, in fact, not gold leaf at all, but rather gold-colored metal leaf, which gradually turns black over time. After careful deliberation, the owners evaluated the long-range economies of the two materials and made the decision to restore with genuine gold leaf and, in the process, took great joy in learning the art of its application from the conservator and participated, in a small way, in some hands-on experience in the restoration.

The gold-leaf detail in the frieze and portions of the living room ceiling acknowledged the golden color of the morning sun reflecting off the lake in the adjacent garden. Charles Greene had understood the subtle natural phenomenon of the golden California morning light and had, in a most creative way, acknowledged this natural feature in the spirit of the living room. The gold leaf had been so delicately handled and muted by its glazing that it harmonized well with the natural-wood finishes and the stained-glass colorations of the living room lighting fixtures. This was a truly special space. Nowhere else in the Greenes' career had they done anything similar. The gold-leaf work had always been a source of pride for Mrs. Blacker and, though it had gradually darkened over the years, was well maintained by the craftsmen whom Henry Greene had check the house periodically.

It therefore came as a shock to Henry, while driving by one day with his daughter and son-in-law several years after Mrs. Blacker's death, to see painters' trucks parked under the porte cochere and the front door open. He asked to stop and went alone into the house only to witness a light green vinyl base paint being rolled over the gold leaf of the frieze and uniformly over the entire ceiling. In his view, the living room was being destroyed. Without looking any further around the house, Henry slowly walked back to the car with tears in his eyes. This, the house that he had monitored for half a century, where he had suggested to Mrs. Blacker that the furniture was so important that she should consider its placement in a museum someday, was being desecrated. Henry never returned to the Blacker House again.

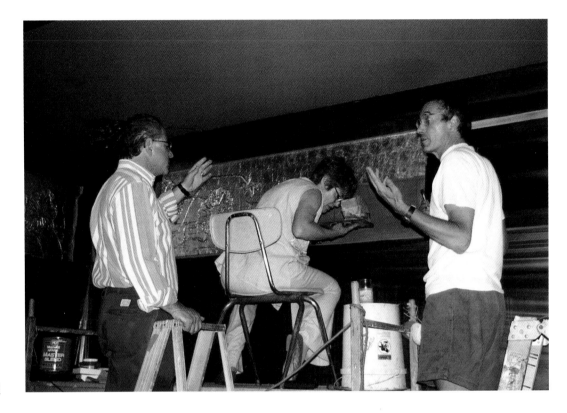

The loss of the lighting fixtures that had been designed by Charles Greene as part of the interior aesthetic left the rooms incomplete. From the beginning, there was never any question that the reinstatement of those designs was as essential as the very purchase of the house itself. During the lengthy restoration, research conducted in various parts of the country assembled the information necessary to address the exact design of each fixture, the type and cut of wood selected, the manner of finite joinery detail, and the subtle color, tone, value, and texture of the stained glass required. Every step was taken to assure that the new creations be equal to the originals—that talent was already a part of the restoration team.

Owner Harvey Knell, left, discusses the process with the conservator as Ellen Knell takes her turn applying gold leaf to the living room frieze.

Bedroom no. 1 restored to the original colors, with re-crafted Greene & Greene light fixtures.

The owners' original restoration plan had always included the reproduction of the original Greene & Greene dining room furniture. However, the desirability of pieces for the other rooms was not intially as clear. It was not until the October 1998 Gamble House exhibition of the restored Blacker House temporarily brought some pieces of the original furniture back to the house that their presence was realized to be so fitting and appropriate to the spaces. Likewise, the rooms without original furniture demonstrated the difficult task of selecting appropriate furniture. Non–Greene & Greene furnishings in certain spaces simply did not complete the unified design.

Following the exhibition to celebrate the end of the main phase of the restoration, there was time to give serious thought to furnishing the Blacker House. The exhibition also provided an opportunity for the interiors to be seen with appropriate Oriental carpets, furniture, and limited accessories. The perception of the scale of the spaces changed. The original light quality was restored by the installation of the original lighting-fixture designs.

The next phase of the restoration would therefore consider reproducing more of the original furniture, designs that British international observer of the Arts & Crafts movement Charles Robert Ashbee described as ". . . without question, the best and most characteristic furniture I have seen in this country."

Top: Restored bedroom no. 4.

Right: Detail of exterior.

Middle: Original carved teak case in the main hall.

Bottom: Restored dining room and Greene & Greene sideboard crafted by James Ipekjian.

The restoration of the Blacker House is, and will always be, a work in process. While the first pieces of furniture have begun to emerge from the shop, neither the owners nor the artisans are in a rush. Photographers are eager to capture the rebirth of this architectural landmark on film to cement its lessons for all time. But none are so eager as to compromise the quality of the decisions and the work itself. As this creative vision of architects Greene & Greene enters its second century, the Blacker House once again possesses principles so fundamental that it continues to convey what Charles Greene described as the art of building spaces and places for living and loving. There is another equation to the future of the Blacker House. There will be added a new energy infused through the presence and values of Ellen and Harvey Knell. Their enlightened belief in the work of these master architects inspired them to invest in those beliefs and to share with the world the artistic genius of architects Charles Sumner Greene and Henry Mather Greene.

ACKNOWLEDGEMENTS

Our thanks go to Ellen and Harvey Knell, whose vision and restoration efforts have made this book possible.

Information from Virginia and Robert R. Blacker, Sarah Boothby, John Boothby, and Matthew Boothby, all members of the Blacker family, has been of great help.

Representatives of distinguished research archives have all been essential. We thank Angela Giral, director, Janet Parks, archivist, and Dan Kany, Avery Architectural and Fine Arts Library, Columbia University in the City of New York; Professor Steven Tobriner, Documents Collection, College of Environmental Design, University of California, Berkeley; Edward R. Bosley, director, Louise Mills, library chairperson, and the volunteers of the Greene & Greene Research Library, The Gamble House, University of Southern California. Also Tania Rizzo, archivist, Kirk Myers, and Mary Borgerding, Pasadena Historical Museum; Stephanie DeWolfe, Mary Jo Winder, Brian Goeken, Jeffrey Cronin, Leon White, and Bill Welden of the Pasadena Permit Center; Bill Reid, Dennis Wong, Department of Water & Power, City of Pasadena; Mary K. B. Carter and Dan McLaughlin, librarians, Pasadena Public Library; Dr. Dan Lewis, curator of American Historical Manuscripts, Melanie Pickett, assistant to the director of the library, Cathy Cherbosque, curator of Prints and Ephemera, Erin Chase, curator, and Jacqueline Dugas, Huntington Library, Art Collections and Botanical Gardens, San Marino, California; Leslie Bowman, Los Angeles County Museum of Art; Nancy McClelland, Peggy Gilges, Christina Geiger, and Christy Woods, Christie's, New York; James Totus, Detroit Institute of the Arts; The Metropolitan Museum of Art, New York; and Professor Emeritus Robert Judson Clark, Princeton University, for years of shared research and inspiring dialogue.

In following the story of the Blackers' early years, research took us to Michigan, Ontario, Canada, and Chicago, Illinois. We are deeply indebted to the following: In Michigan—Steve Harold, director, Manistee County Historical Museum; Manistee Public Library; Debbie Berryman, director, Buchanan Public Library. In Brantford, Ontario,

Canada—George, Lorraine, and Lee Skitch, beloved owners of the original Blacker house; former owner Ruth Bryant; Marion Silverthorn, a distant Blacker family relative; Ernie Turvey; Michael O'Byrne, Heritage Mount Pleasant; Peter Marsh, administrator, Blacker Trust; June and Thomas Hird, owners of the former Blacker farm; Brantford Land Registry office; Brian Wood, curator, Alexander Bell Homestead. In Chicago—Steve Peters, Tim Samuelson, Chicago Historical Society; Lora Campana, Chicago Athletic Club; and Frank Lipo, executive director, Historical Society of Oak Park & River Forest.

Members of the Greene family continue to assist in providing valuable information and we are grateful to the Greenes' children: Gordon and Betty Greene, Ruth Greene, Isabelle (Greene) and Alan R. McElwain; and grandchildren: Nancy Glass, Virginia Hales, Isabelle Greene, Alan G. McElwain, and Alice Cory.

To all members of our families—Heinz, Makinson, Pitt—we express our appreciation for their unstinting support and understanding.

Many individuals have been important to this work in a variety of ways, and for their individual roles we thank Brian Aamoth, Jennifer Aniston, Cathy Considine, Barbara Ealy, Eastman Kodak Co., Doris and Constantine Gertmenian, members of the Peter and John Hall families: Robert, Nadine, Gregson, Chad, Mark, Gary, Betsy, Alice, Walter, Marilyn, and Doris; Mark Henderson, The Getty Center, Los Angeles, California; Max and Margery Hill for their many years of friendship and love of the Blacker House; Katie Ipekjian; The Judson Studios, Horace, Walter and David Judson; Virginia Ernst Kazor; Joan Kaas, member of the Emil Lange family; Kristin Leachman, Robert Leary, B. Lepejian, Richard Malchar, James Marrin, Janeen Marrin, Erica Marrin, Virginia and Howard Martens, Dennis McGuire, Michael Meisinger, Consolidated Media Services; Nikon; Robert Perkins, Michael Sanville, Eugene Selger, Sinar, Boyd Smith, Bruce Smith and Yoshiko Yamamoto, Dr. Robert Wark, Robert W. Winter, Stephen and Lisa Woods, Lloyd Yost, L. Morgan Yost, and Winogene Yost.

Special acknowledgement to Margaret McCord for her thoughtful editing; Gibbs and Catherine Smith, Madge Baird, Linda Nimori, Christopher Robbins, Glenn Jensen, Monica Millward, Sue Carabine, and Marty Lee of Gibbs Smith, Publisher, for believing in this book; to J. Scott Knudsen and Mardi Knudsen for computer assistance; and to Daniel Nelson Bube and Alvaro Zepeda for new drawings.

For technical assistance with the design layout and computer wizardry we are indebted to Jeremy Davis, Brian Hinton, R. Sky Kogachi, and Alvaro R. Zepeda.

And finally, our sincere thanks for the support and encouragement of those who have been closest to this project throughout: Madge Baird, Scott Randell Charles, Ann T. Heinz, Donald C. Hensman, David D. Judson, Paula Makinson Stewart, and Brad Pitt.

RESTORATION TEAM

In 1994 Ellen and Harvey Knell assembled a group of artisans to carry out the faithful restoration of the Blacker House. The following contributed to that effort:

Accounting, Bookkeeping: Julia Lyman
Art Conservation / Gold Leaf: Patrice Pinaquy, Lucien Retourné
City of Pasadena: Ray Chen, Jeff Cronin, Bob J. Fowler, Robert Fu,
    Brian Goeken, Alex Khoury, Vera Lichlyter, Felix Obamogie,
    Denver Miller, Bill Reid, William T. Wang, Mary Jo Winder,
    Jerry Wood, Dennis Wong.
Earthquake Retrofit: Eagle Builders, Tim Gohr, Jeff Smith
Electrical: Craft Electric, Edward Schwartz, Damon Fuller
Furniture: James M. Ipekjian
Flooring: Youngs Floor Co, Edward P. Young, Edward P. Young Jr.
Hazardous Materials: Abatec Group, Dennis Hanna
Insulation: San Gabriel Insulation, Rick Dubin, Paul Sevilla,
    Alberto Camarena, and Scott Fielding
Landscaping: Rosalio Terrones, Paul Terrones, and Angel Terrones.
Lighting Consultant: Barbara Hershan Hirsch
Lighting—Exterior Lanterns: Buffalo Studios, Greg Bowman,
    Tony Smith, Cliff Mathieson
Lighting—Interior Fixtures: James Ipekjian; Ben, Garo, and Jack Ipekjian
Art Glass: John Hamm, Debbie Rupe, Sam Smith
Masonry: Lief S. Petersen & Sons, Inc., Chris Petersen, Moen Petersen,
    Michael Petersen
Mechanical Engineering, HVAC: Johnson Associates, Russel A. Johnson
Installation: Skillman HVAC, Robert Skillman; Roth Bros.
Paint Removal & Finish Preparation: Charles Barrett, Manny Estrada,
    Jesse Garcia, Eddie Orosco
Painting & Wood Finishing: Brian Miller Associates, Brian Miller,
    German Lucero, Carlos Arroyo
Plastering: Randy Ayers, B. J. Robinson
Plating: Model Plating Co., Dick Fratello
Plumbing, R. C. Ives Plumbing, Ron Ives, James Laite; Georges
    Pipe & Supply Co., Rick Brandley, Skip Stiver
    Vintage Plumbing: Donald G. Hooper
Roofing: William H. Lavey & Associates, William H. Lavey,
    Gunnar Kirchhoff, Abraham Cortez, Eric Langston, Richard Ballard,
    Don Sandling, Fidel Curiel
Screens: J & L Screens, Javier Martinez
Security Systems: Robert De Lima, Doug Brusche, Blair Wonderly
Sheet Metals: Eagle Rock Sheet Metal, William Gillan, Al Gillan,
    Roy Deller, Henry Mejia; C & J Sheet Metal, S & S Sheet Metal,
    Jim Slaughter, John Slaughter
Shakes & Siding: Robert Warren Roofing, Robert A. Warren,
    John P. Warren
Sound & Imaging Systems: Darrell Copeland, Vincent A. Van Haaff
Structural Engineering: Roselund Engineering, Nels Roselund
Terrazzo: Arcadian Flooring, Ted Lambros
Tilework: Quarry Tile Co., Thomas Sawyer

Tiler: Ralph R. McIntosh
Woodworking:
    Carpentry: Paul Boehm, Chesney Construction, Dennis Chesney;
    Green II Builders, Jack Green, Bill Friend, Mike Zirbes;
    Ipekjian Custom Woodwork, James M. Ipekjian;
    Lawrence Construction, Larry Lee
    Cabinetwork: John Benriter; A. Fortner Woodshop,
    Anthony Fortner; Ronin Builders, Robert Clemens,
    Scott C. Lightfoot, Michael W. Banks
Wrought Iron: J B Welding, Juan Barajas

Restoration Architect: Randell L. Makinson
Project Manager: William J. Searle
Technical Advisor: James M. Ipekjian

ILLUSTRATION CREDITS

The following individuals and institutions have made illustrative materials available for this book:

Photographers

■ Matthew Robert Boothby, © 2000, 116 t.

■ Jeremy M. Davis, © 2000, 45 br.

■ Thomas A. Heinz, AIA, photographer, © 2000 RLM Associates, ii, iv, vii, xi, 1, 3, 5, 7 b, 12, 26, 27, 31 t, 35, 36, 38 t, 40 r, 42, 43, 44, 45 t & bl, 46, 47, 48 tr, 49, 50, 51, 52, 53, 54, 55, 56, 57, 58, 59, 60, 61, 62, 63, 64, 65, 66, 67 t, 68 tl & tm & b, 69, 70, 74, 75, 80, 83, 100, 102, 105, 108, 113 t, 114, 115 b, 117, 119 t, 120, 121, 123, 124, 125, 126, 127, 128.

■ Ellen Knell, © 2000, Jacket back flap t

■ Randell L. Makinson, Hon, AIA, © 2000, xii, 4, 40 tl, 68 tr, 73 b, 79 tr & tl, 81 b, 107, 110, 111, 112, 113 b, 115 t, 119 b.

■ Brian Miller © 2000, 122.

■ Brad Pitt, © 2000, vi, 84, 85, 86, 87, 88, 89, 90, 91, 92, 93, 94, 95, 96, 97, 98, 99, 129, 131.

Archival Sources

■ Thomas A. Heinz archive, 1875 Map of the County of Brant, Ontario, Canada, drawn by C. L. Smith, 2.

■ Randell L. Makinson archive, 20, 31 b, 32 l, 33, 34, 41 tr, 48 br, 77 b, 116 bl, 118 l; Charles Sumner Greene photographs, 22, 24, 25; Maynard Parker photographs, 48 l, 67 b, 79 bl.

■ *The Architectural Forum,* October 1948, 21.

■ *The Craftsman,* October 1907, 41 tm.

■ Avery Architectural and Fine Arts Library, Columbia University in the City of New York, 30.

■ Greene & Greene Library, The Gamble House, USC, Pasadena, California, 17, 23 t & b, 29 t, 38 b, 72, 73, 76, 77 t, 78 b, 79 br, 81 t, 104; Leroy Hulbert photographs, 38, 73, 76, 81 t.

■ Huntington Library, Art Galleries and Botanical Gardens, San Marino, California, 15.

■ Manistee County Historical Museum, Manistee, Michigan, 6, 7 tl, 8 b, 9 b, 10–11.

■ Pasadena Public Library, Pasadena, California, *Pasadena Daily News,* 1 January 1911, 14; *Architectural Record,* October 1906.

Other Sources

■ Blacker family, 7 tm & tr, 8 tl & tr, 9 tl & r, 11.

■ Boothby family, Leroy Hulbert photograph, 28.

■ Christie's, New York, 78 t.

■ T. H. Robsjohn-Gibbings, *Homes of the Brave* (with drawings by Mary Petty), Alfred A. Knopf, New York, 1954, 132.

Drawings

■ Daniel Nelson Bube, 40 tm.

■ Alvaro R. Zepeda, 116 br, 118 r.

Drawing Enhancement

■ Jeremy Michael Davis, 41 tm.

Key:

t = top

m = middle

b = bottom

l = left

r = right

COLOPHON

This book and jacket
were designed by
Randell L. Makinson and
Thomas A. Heinz.

This book was
typeset in
Adobe Garamond.

Printing and binding
executed in Hong Kong
by Toppan Printing.

FOR CHARLES SUMNER CeREENE
WIITH BEST WIISHES .

T. H. Holgshn-Tibbings

T. H. Robsjohn-Gibbings was a furniture designer for the John Widdicomb Company of Grand Rapids, Michigan, an author of three books on antiques, architecture, and art, and a lifelong admirer of the work of Greene & Greene. Illustration from his book Homes of the Brave.